A NEW OWNER'S
GUIDE TO
BOSTON TERRIERS

JG-153

T.F.H. Publications, Inc.
One TFH Plaza
Third and Union Avenues
Neptune City, NJ 07753

05 06 07 08 09   5 7 9 8 6 4

This book has been published with the intent to provide accurate and authoritative information in regard to the subject matter within. While every precaution has been taken in preparation of this book, the publisher and author assume no responsibility for errors or omissions. Neither is any liability assumed for damages resulting from the use of the information herein.

ISBN 0-7938-2802-3

www.tfhpublications.com

A New Owner's Guide to
Boston Terriers

Bob & Eleanor Candland

Contents

2004 Edition

**The Boston Terrier's unique look
and fun personality attract people
to the breed.**

**The Boston Terrier is the ultimate
companion dog.**

It's hard to resist an adorable Boston Terrier puppy.

A purebred Boston pup should look just like his parents.

The energetic Boston Terrier loves to have fun with his owner.

HISTORY and Origin of the Boston Terrier

THE BREED'S ADAM AND EVE

The history of most breeds of dog is, at best, shrouded in mystery. Most often, neither the exact location nor the specific individuals involved in creating the breed are known. The history of the Boston Terrier, on the other hand, is by and large a matter of documented fact. In 1865, one Robert C. Hooper, a resident of Boston, Massachusetts, imported a dog from England, the country from which he had immigrated. While still living there, Hooper grew fond of the many bulldog and terrier crossbreeds that had been developed and were highly popular in that country: He decided to have such a dog in his new country of residence, and in that same year, his purchase arrived. The dog became known as Hooper's Judge.

Di Amore's Omaggio a Leonora gets her distinctive look from the Bullbaiter-Bulldog crosses in the 19th century.

There is no doubt that Judge was all-English—both sides of his crossed pedigree represented the distinctive breeds that were developed there. But Hooper's Judge was to become the Boston Terrier breed's "Adam," and his only known mate, Burnett's Gyp, was to be his "Eve." Both Judge and Gyp (also known as Burnett's Kate) traced their ancestry back to the bull and terrier crosses, so it is interesting to take a brief look back at where those breeds came from and what they were like.

The modern Boston Terrier's ancestors can be traced back to English Bulldogs, once used as fierce dogs that battled bulls for sport.

THE BULLBAITERS

The tribes that occupied northern Europe were known to have kept large, fierce dogs of the Mastiff type. These dogs had descended from the wolves that inhabited the great mountain range stretching from east to west across Asia and Europe. The Romans bred these Mastiff-type dogs to fight in the arena against bulls, bears, and other wild animals. These dogs were known as Alains or Alaunts until the Middle Ages. In Britain, these same large and fierce dogs became known as bandogs because ropes, chains, or bands were employed to keep them under control.

The ferocious dogs were the forerunners of the Bulldog, which was developed through manipulative breeding in England. Their original purpose in England was to assist butchers in controlling the savage bulls from which food for the table would be gleaned. It was commonly believed that meat of a much more tender and nutritious quality could be had from bulls that had been worried by these bandogs prior to butchering, rather than meat that came from bulls immediately slaughtered.

The dogs were developed with short legs and heavy bodies that served to keep them out of the way of the bulls' horns. Eventually, man adapted these tough dogs so they could participate in a savage sport that challenged the dog against a bull. The dogs' owners took pride in seeing who owned the most ferocious dog that was most capable of bringing the bull to the ground. Thus was born the sport of bullbaiting.

In these contests, the dog was to grab the bull by the nose when the tethered bull attempted to impale the dog on its horns. The dog was to hold on to the bull, with no regard to his own personal injury, until the bull finally expired from loss of blood and oxygen deprivation.

The undershot jaw of the Bulldog enabled him to clamp onto the bull's nose with such a vice-like grip that it was impossible for the bull to dislodge the dog. The dog's heavy body weight and low center of gravity, combined with his sheer grit and determination, could eventually bring the bull to ground. These same characteristics came to distinguish the Bulldog for all time to come.

It was from the duties assigned to these tenacious dogs that the characteristics that distinguish the Bulldog of today were developed. A head of great size provided the power required of the jaws to secure the iron grip on the bull's nose. The undershot and upward curving conformation of the muzzle not only provided as secure a hold as could be had, but it also pushed the dog's nose back from the end of the muzzle. Thus, even with jaws clamped tight, the dog's nose was free to take in needed air.

Fortunately, bullbaiting was banned in England by an act of Parliament in 1835, but whenever British dog breeders sought tenacity, they looked to the Bulldog. The breed was dauntless but tractable. He had all the courage, but none of the ferocity toward man that he did when pitted against other animals.

THE TERRIERS

In sharp contrast to the low-stationed, determined, and rather cumbersome Bulldog was Britain's other creation—the terrier. Most terriers seem to have descended from the spitz-type dog that existed throughout the European countries. They were used as "ratters," and assigned duties that always demanded speed and rapid response. Although terriers took many physical forms, without exception they were acutely alert and agile and had hair-trigger responses.

When the British found need for a dog with tenacity, body strength, and determination that was also speedy and agile, it is easy to see why they looked to the bulldog-terrier cross to produce it.

Mr. Hooper's Judge

Judge was mostly bulldog, yet his terrier ancestry was also apparent. Whether Judge's heritage was contributed to by a white bull terrier or by the English terrier (extinct) is unknown, but the late breed authority Vincent G. Perry always claimed it was the latter, in that the English terrier came in two colors: white and black-and-tan. Perry believed that the rich, dark color of the Boston Terrier was attributable to the breed's ancient black-and-tan English terrier ancestry.

Judge was blessed with an amiable yet courageous spirit. He was of stocky build, very square and blocky, and weighed 32 pounds. His mouth was reported as being slightly undershot, and he was colored dark brindle with a white collar and narrow facial blaze.

Edward Burnett of nearby Southboro, Massachusetts, admired Judge and decided to breed his Burnett's Gyp (a.k.a Burnett's Kate) to the stalwart English import. Gyp was all white and lower-stationed than Judge, but possessed a similarly blocky head with a three-quarter tail. Her weight was approximately 20 pounds.

History records only one offspring from this mating—a male named Well's Eph. He was said to have lacked any of the attractive

One of the Boston's forefathers was Hooper's Judge, a bulldog and terrier cross.

characteristics of his parents, Judge and Gyp. In fact, whenever reference is made to Eph, the chronicler makes a point of the dog's lack of beauty, even suggesting ugliness. He was dark brindle with white markings on his head and a small amount of white on each foot.

As unattractive as he was, Eph was able to produce a much more handsome son known as Barnard's Tom. Tom was first to exhibit any of the quality and refinement that was to typify the latter-day Boston Terrier. He also had a characteristic that fascinated the dog men of his time—a very short and twisted screw tail. Tom was heavily bred because of his good looks and because of his unique screw tail. He was put to females of bulldog and terrier cross, terrier and French bulldog cross, and some say even to females that had descended from boxer crosses.

Tom was owned by John P. Bernard, a Boston resident who owned a highly successful livery stable in the city, which was a gathering place for other stablemen and dog fanciers. These men liked Tom's offspring, which exhibited their sire's compact shape and great spirit.

The stable was often the site of pit fighting, where one dog was set upon another. Up until that time, the cruel sport had still not

Am. Can. Ch. Zuran's Daisy May 'N Hi Society, owned by Cynthia J. Davis of Hi-Society Boston Terriers.

Nordic Ch. Oelandica's Mrs. Quickly displays the compact build and alert stance characteristic of the breed.

been outlawed. The descendants of Eph and Tom fared well in these events, but what the pit fighting supporters found equally attractive about the dogs was the fact that they were amiable and trustworthy with all humans.

Line breeding and inbreeding began to take place, and a definite look, along with a reduction in size, made the dogs increasingly popular. Soon the dog that had only enjoyed popularity among stablemen found acceptance with the general public.

This Boston-bred dog called upon the admirable qualities of every one of his bulldog and terrier ancestors and, as a result, found as much favor in a lady's drawing room as he did with the master of the household. The dog proved to have traits that appealed to all people—affectionate lap dog, vermin warden, watchdog, and a no-nonsense scrapper.

In 1890, Charles F. Leland, a Harvard University student and fancier of the breed, secured the names of 40 other men in the Boston area who shared his interest. He sent them all an invitation to form a club that would create a standard for the breed and generally champion the breed's cause. Although each of the 40 wanted a standard that would fit their own treasured dog, in the end, a very comprehensive standard was formulated. That standard still bears influence on the one used by fanciers of the breed today.

By 1891, the breed's sterling character and great popularity had risen so high, his fanciers began to keep breeding records, and any crossing with other breeds was strongly discouraged. The fanciers of this breed alternately referred to him as the "round-headed bulldog," "Boston bulldog," "toy bulldog," and "bullet head." Regardless of what they called the little dog, his fans were fiercely loyal and sought American Kennel Club approval as a true breed.

The bulldog fancy was extremely powerful in the AKC at that time, and they bitterly opposed acceptance of the breed that they referred to as "this Boston-bred mongrel." At that time, the AKC was in its infancy and was doing its utmost to establish dominance over all purebred dogs. Petty rivalries and jealousies created arbitrary decisions in the organization, and opposition to Boston's favorite dog was one of these seemingly groundless edicts.

Dedication on the part of the breed's fanciers eventually prevailed and, in 1893, the AKC relented. The breed, newly christened as the

The author, Bob Candland, pictured with Ch. El Bo's Rudy is a Dandy, one of the all-time greatest winning Boston Terriers in the history of the breed.

The shape and coloring of the Boston Terrier's head is what distinguishes him from other breeds.

Boston Terrier, was admitted to the studbook. The breed had won its most important fight.

The first Boston Terrier registered with the AKC was Hector, whelped in July of 1891. He is described as brindle and white in color and sired by Bixby's Tony. Hector's dam is listed as Dimple, and he was bred by Geo. H. Huse of Boston, Massachusetts, and owned by Joseph Al Locke of Chicago, Illinois.

The breed's first AKC champion was a female named Topsy, but Heilborn's Raffles and Ringmaster (a.k.a Sport IV) is credited as fixing the type of Boston Terrier admired today. Raffles contributed his small size, black color, and great eye and expression to his offspring. Raffles lacked markings, but it was to the breed's good, in that many specimens had far too much white, and others were splashed with white all over their bodies. Ringmaster changed the eye of the breed from the narrow terrier eye to the round expressive eye by which the breed is now so well distinguished.

The compact size and easygoing disposition of the little dog from Boston moved forward in popularity and registrations with amazing speed. From 1920 to 1963, the breed stood within the top ten of all breeds registered with the AKC.

Although the Boston no longer enjoys the enormous popularity he once did, he continues to maintain a respectable place near the top half of all breeds registered annually with the AKC. He will never slip beyond first place in the hearts of those who have owned this enchanting companion breed.

As proof of the love owners have for this breed, fanciers in the state of Massachusetts initiated a movement to have the Boston Terrier become the official state dog. Edward King, the state's governor at the time, elevated the Boston to this position officially in 1979. Governor King had owned a Boston Terrier named Skippy when he was a boy.

BEFORE YOU BUY a Boston Terrier

The Boston Terrier has a wealth of positive characteristics and undeniable appeal. Boston Terrier puppies are the subjects of thousands of picture-postcards, greeting cards, and calendars each year. There is nothing more endearing than that angelic, little Boston pup looking up with those big "won't you please adopt me?" eyes.

However, in addition to being cute, Boston puppies are living, breathing creatures that are entirely dependent upon their human owners for everything once they leave their mother and littermates. It is for this very reason that people who are anticipating owning a Boston should give serious thought to the decision.

Buying any dog, especially a puppy, before someone is absolutely sure that he or she wants to make the commitment can be a serious mistake. The prospective dog owner must clearly understand the amount of time and work involved in dog ownership. Failure to understand the extent of this commitment is one of the primary reasons that so many unwanted canines end their lives in animal shelters.

There are some very important conditions that must be considered before anyone contemplates the purchase of a dog. One of the first questions to be answered is whether the person who will ultimately be responsible for the dog's care and well-being actually wants a dog.

All too often, it is the parents of the household who must shoulder the responsibility of the family dog's day-to-day care. Having pets is a wonderful way to teach children responsibility, but parents should remember that the enthusiasm that inspires children to promise anything in order to have a new puppy might quickly wane. Who will take care of the puppy once the novelty wears off? Does that person want a dog?

Desire to own a dog aside, does the lifestyle of the family actually provide for responsible dog ownership? If the entire family is away from early morning to late at night, who will provide for all of a puppy's needs? Feeding, exercise, and outdoor access cannot be provided if no one is home.

Another important factor to consider is whether the breed is suitable for the person or the family with which he will be living.

The Boston Terrier's unique look, sparkling personality, and interesting history are what attracts people to the breed.

Some breeds can handle the rough-and-tumble play of young children. Some cannot. On the other hand, some dogs are so large and clumsy, especially as puppies, that they could easily and unintentionally injure an infant.

Then, too, there is the matter of hair. A luxurious coat is certainly beautiful to behold, but all that hair takes a great deal of care. At first thought, it would seem that a smooth-coated dog like the Boston would eliminate this problem. Not so, as we will see. While there is no long hair or clipping to

Before you bring a Boston into your home, make sure he will fit in your family and your lifestyle.

contend with, there is a great deal for the owner of any smooth-coated dog to do to keep his or her companion happy and healthy.

As great as claims are for any breed's intelligence and trainability, remember the new dog must be taught every household rule which he is to observe. Some dogs catch on more quickly than others, and puppies are just as inclined to forget or disregard lessons as young human children are.

CASE FOR THE PUREBRED DOG

All puppies are cute, but not all puppies grow up to be the picture of what we, as humans, find attractive. What one person sees as beautiful is not necessarily pleasing to another. It is almost impossible to determine what a mixed-breed puppy will look like as an adult, nor will it be possible to determine if the mixed-breed puppy's temperament is suitable for the person or family that wishes to own him. If the puppy grows up to be too big, too stubborn, or too active for the owner, what then will happen to him?

Boston Terriers both young and old love the outdoors and need plenty of exercise.

Size and temperament can vary, to a degree, even within a purebred breed. Still, selective breeding over many generations has produced dogs that give the would-be owner reasonable assurance of what the purebred puppy will look and act like as an adult. Purebred puppies will grow up to look like their adult relatives and they will behave pretty much like the rest of their family. Any dog, mixed breed or not, has the potential to be a loving companion. However, a purebred dog offers reasonable insurance that he will not only suit the owner's lifestyle, but the person's aesthetic demands as well.

WHO SHOULD OWN A BOSTON TERRIER?

What kind of a person should own a Boston Terrier? Perhaps this question is best answered by stating, first and foremost, that a Boston owner must be a person with *patience and understanding.*

The Boston is a very intelligent breed, but these dogs have a lot of interests and, without proper training, may well decide to pursue those interests regardless of how many commands you might give. A short-tempered person is not the right kind of owner for a Boston.

A securely fenced yard is an absolute must for the Boston owner, or he or she must be prepared to be with their dog and have him on leash each time the dog is allowed outdoors. This applies in the hottest, coldest, or wettest of weather.

Also, for many reasons, the Boston is an indoor dog. Because of his short coat, he does not like, nor can he tolerate, extremes in weather. The Boston has a short, flat nose, and the breed should not be exposed to excessive heat, as high temperatures can cause death. Similarly, the breed is not equipped to withstand extremely cold or wet weather.

On the other hand, the Boston is generally a very healthy dog. There is not nearly as much work involved in keeping the breed clean and healthy as with some other breeds, but this does not mean you can leave your Boston Terrier to his own devices when it comes to hygiene. Ears, eyes, mouth, and feet need regular inspection, and though the Boston's coat is short, he will still benefit from a regular good brushing or rub down with a rough towel.

A BREEDER CHECKLIST

Just as the buyer should have a checklist to guide him or her in locating a responsible breeder, most responsible breeders have criteria that a buyer must meet before they would be considered an ideal candidate to purchase one of their puppies. The following list presents some of the issues that prospective Boston owners should consider.

1. Security is a must. Though Boston Terriers are usually described as being loyal, most Bostons could be just as happy anywhere, as long as he is fed, loved, petted, and has a couch or chair on which to sleep. Bostons love people, and therefore will often accept an invitation to take a stroll with a passing child or even hop into the car of a total stranger. For this reason, the Boston owner must have a securely fenced yard.

2. A Boston Terrier should only go into a home where everyone welcomes him. Owning a Boston Terrier takes the cooperation of everyone in the household, and no Boston will be completely happy or healthy in an environment that does not fully accept him as a member of the family.

3. Boston Terriers should not go into a home where children are solely responsible for the dog's care. Mature Bostons are stoic and will take almost any abuse from a child; therefore parental supervision

A responsible breeder will ask a prospective owner many questions in order to determine whether the Boston Terrier is the right dog for that household.

is an absolute must. While the best of children can love and care for their dogs, they are not always capable of understanding or remembering the special care dog ownership entails. Boston puppies are small and fragile. Children must be taught how to carefully handle and care for these little ones.

4. Boston Terriers should not go into a home where the buyer "wants to get into breeding." Breeding Boston Terriers takes a great deal of time, patience, and hard work. It takes a long time to understand what kind of stock is suitable for breeding and an even longer time to learn the intricacies of breeding, whelping, and rearing a litter of Bostons. There are many complications that must be anticipated, and only a sincere, responsible person interested in improving the breed is suitable for this purpose.

STANDARD for the Boston Terrier

General Appearance—The Boston Terrier is a lively, highly intelligent, smooth coated, short-headed, compactly built, short-tailed, well balanced dog, brindle, seal or black in color and evenly marked with white. The head is in proportion to the size of the dog and the expression indicates a high degree of intelligence.

The body is rather short and well knit, the limbs strong and neatly turned, the tail is short and no feature is so prominent that the dog appears badly proportioned. The dog conveys an impression of determination, strength and activity, with style of a high order; carriage easy and graceful. A proportionate combination of "Color and White Markings" is a particularly distinctive feature of a representative specimen.

"Balance, Expression, Color and White Markings" should be given particular consideration in determining the relative value of GENERAL APPEARANCE to other points.

The Boston Terrier is a well-balanced dog with distinctive black-and-white markings.

The Boston Terrier's has large, dark eyes and a kind, alert expression. Ch. OJ's First Class Mi Manacci, owned by Cynthia J. Pagurski.

Size, Proportion, Substance—Weight is divided by classes as follows: Under 15 pounds; 15 pounds and under 20 pounds; 20 pounds and not to exceed 25 pounds. The length of leg must balance with the length of body to give the Boston Terrier its striking square appearance. The Boston Terrier is a sturdy dog and must not appear to be either spindly or coarse. The bone and muscle must be in proportion as well as an enhancement to the dog's weight and structure. *Fault:* Blocky or chunky in appearance.

Influence of Sex. In a comparison of specimens of each sex, the only evident difference is a slight refinement in the bitch's conformation.

Head—The *skull* is square, flat on top, free from wrinkles, cheeks flat, brow abrupt and the stop well defined. The ideal Boston Terrier *expression* is alert and kind, indicating a high degree of intelligence. This is a most important characteristic of the breed. The *eyes* are wide apart, large and round and dark in color. The eyes are set square in the skull and the outside corners are on a line with the cheeks as viewed from the front. *Disqualify:* Eyes blue in color or any trace of blue. The *ears* are small, carried erect, either natural or cropped to conform to the shape of the head and situated as near to the corners of the skull as possible.

The *muzzle* is short, square, wide and deep and in proportion to the skull. It is free from wrinkles, shorter in length than in width or depth; not exceeding in length approximately one-third of the length of the skull. The muzzle from stop to end of the nose is parallel to the top of the skull.

The *nose* is black and wide, with a well defined line between the nostrils. *Disqualify:* Dudley nose.

The *jaw* is broad and square with short regular teeth. The bite is even or sufficiently undershot to square the muzzle. The chops are of good depth, but not pendulous, completely covering the teeth when the mouth is closed. *Serious Fault:* Wry mouth.

Head Faults: Eyes showing too much white or haw. Pinched or wide nostrils. Size of ears out of proportion to the size of the head. *Serious Head Faults:* Any showing of the tongue or teeth when the mouth is closed.

Neck, Topline and Body—The length of *neck* must display an image of balance to the total dog. It is slightly arched, carrying the head gracefully and setting neatly into the shoulders. The *back* is just short enough to square the body. The *topline* is level and the

A purebred Boston Terrier puppy should look exactly like his parents.

rump curves slightly to the set-on of the tail. The *chest* is deep with good width, ribs well sprung and carried well back to the loins. The body should appear short. The *tail* is set on low, short, fine and tapering, straight or screw and must not be carried above the horizontal. (Note: The preferred tail does not exceed in length more than one-quarter the distance from set-on to hock.) ***Disqualify:*** Docked tail.

Body Faults: Gaily carried tail. ***Serious Body Faults:*** Roach back, sway back, slab-sided.

Forequarters—The *shoulders* are sloping and well laid back, which allows for the Boston Terrier's stylish movement. The *elbows* stand neither in nor out. The *forelegs* are set moderately wide apart and on a line with the upper tip of the shoulder blades. The forelegs are straight in bone with short, strong pasterns. The dewclaws may be removed. The *feet* are small, round and compact, turned neither in nor out, with well arched toes and short nails. ***Faults:*** Legs lacking in substance; splay feet.

Hindquarters—The *thighs* are strong and well muscled, bent at the stifles and set true. The *hocks* are short to the feet, turning

The Boston Terrier is a sure-footed dog whose stance indicates grace and power.

The tight, compact body of the Boston Terrier contributes to his overall balanced and square appearance.

neither in nor out, with a well defined hock joint. The *feet* are small and compact with short nails. *Fault:* Straight in stifle.

Gait—The gait of the Boston Terrier is that of a sure footed, straight gaited dog, forelegs and hind legs moving straight ahead in line with perfect rhythm, each step indicating grace and power. *Gait Faults:* There will be no rolling, paddling, or weaving, when gaited. Hackney gait. *Serious Gait Faults:* Any crossing movement, either front or rear.

Coat—The coat is short, smooth, bright and fine in texture.

Color and Markings—Brindle, seal, or black with white markings. Brindle is preferred ONLY if all other qualities are equal. (Note: SEAL DEFINED. Seal appears black except it has a red cast when viewed in the sun or bright light.) *Disqualify:* Solid black, solid brindle or solid seal without required white markings. Gray or liver colors.

Required Markings: White muzzle band, white blaze between the eyes, white forechest.

Desired Markings: White muzzle band, even white blaze between the eyes and over the head, white collar, white forechest, white on part or whole of forelegs and hind legs below the hocks. (Note: A representative specimen should not be penalized for not possessing "Desired Markings.")

A dog with a preponderance of white on the head or body must possess sufficient merit otherwise to counteract its deficiencies.

Temperament—The Boston Terrier is a friendly and lively dog. The breed has an excellent disposition and a high degree of intelligence, which makes the Boston Terrier an incomparable companion.

Summary—The clean-cut short backed body of the Boston Terrier coupled with the unique characteristics of his square head and jaw, and his striking markings have resulted in a most dapper and charming American original: The Boston Terrier.

SCALE OF POINTS

General Appearance	10
Expression	10
Head (Muzzle, Jaw, Bite, Skull & Stop)	15
Eyes	5
Ears	5
Neck, Topline, Body & Tail	15
Forequarters	10
Hindquarters	10
Feet	5
Color, Coat & Markings	5
Gait	10
TOTAL	100

DISQUALIFICATIONS

Eyes blue in color or any trace of blue.

Dudley nose.

Docked tail.

Solid black, solid brindle, or solid seal without required white markings.

Gray or liver colors.

Approved January 9, 1990
Effective February 28, 1990

SELECTING the Right Boston Terrier for You

The Boston Terrier puppy you bring into your home will be your best friend and a member of your family for many years to come. The average well-bred and well-cared-for Boston is apt to live far longer than many of the large breeds. A Boston Terrier can easily live to be between 12 and 14 years old.

Early care and sound breeding is vital to the longevity of your Boston. Therefore, it is of the utmost importance that the dog you select has had every opportunity to begin life in a healthy, stable environment and comes from stock that is both physically and temperamentally sound. The only way you can be assured of all this is to go directly to a breeder who has consistently produced Bostons of this kind over the years.

A breeder earns his or her reputation through a well-planned breeding program that has been governed by rigid selectivity. Selective breeding programs are aimed at maintaining the breed's many fine qualities and keeping the breed free of as many genetic weaknesses as possible. Responsible Boston breeders protect their tremendous investment of time and money by basing their breeding programs on the healthiest, most representative breeding stock

Early care and sound breeding is vital to the good health and temperament of a Boston Terrier puppy.

Selective breeding programs are aimed at maintaining the breed's many fine qualities and keeping them free from genetic problems or inherited health conditions.

available. These breeders provide each following generation with the very best care, sanitation, and nutrition available.

Governing kennel clubs of the world maintain lists of local breed clubs and breeders that can lead a prospective Boston buyer to responsible breeders of quality stock. If you are not sure of where to find an established breeder in your area, we strongly recommend getting in touch with your local or national kennel club for recommendations. Many good pet shops also carry lists of local, responsible breeders.

Finding a local breeder will allow you to visit the breeder's home or kennel, inspect the facility, and, in many cases, see a puppy's parents and other relatives. Good breeders are always willing and able to discuss any problems that might exist in the breed and how they should be dealt with.

If there aren't any Boston Terrier breeders in your immediate area, taking the time and exerting the effort to plan a trip to a reputable breeder's home or kennel would be well worth your while. If this is not possible, some breeders will arrange to ship a puppy to you by air. The shipping details are best discussed with the breeder you speak to, as they differ from person to person, and different states have different shipping regulations.

Never hesitate to ask the breeder you visit or speak with on the phone any questions or concerns you might have relative to Boston Terrier ownership. Responsible breeders, in turn, ask many questions of those who anticipate purchasing a puppy from them. Good breeders are just as interested in placing their Boston puppies in a loving and safe environment as you are in obtaining a happy, healthy puppy.

Not all good breeders maintain large kennels. In fact, you are just as apt to find quality Bostons that come from the homes of small hobby breeders who keep only a few dogs and have litters only occasionally. The names of these people are just as likely to appear on the recommended lists from kennel clubs as the larger kennels that maintain many dogs. Hobby breeders are equally dedicated to breeding quality dogs. A factor in favor of hobby breeders is their distinct advantage of being able to raise their puppies in a home environment with all the accompanying personal attention and socialization.

Again, it is important that both the buyer and seller ask questions. Be extremely suspicious of anyone who is willing to sell you a Boston Terrier puppy with no questions asked.

Do not just show up on the doorstep of a breeder's home or kennel. Call ahead and make an appointment at a convenient time so that you will be expected and not rushed.

Recognizing a Healthy Puppy

Boston breeders seldom release their puppies until they are at least 10 to 12 weeks of age and have been given at least one of their puppy inoculations. By the time the litter is eight weeks old, the

Good breeding will be evident in the puppy's curious attitude and overall healthy appearance.

From the very beginning, proper health care and socialization is essential to your Boston Terrier's long and happy life.

puppies are entirely weaned and no longer nursing on the mother. While puppies are nursing, they have a degree of immunity from diseases from their mother. Once they have stopped nursing, they become highly susceptible to many infectious diseases. A number of these diseases can be transmitted on the hands and clothing of humans. Therefore, it is extremely important that your puppy is current on all the shots he must have for his age.

A healthy Boston puppy is a happy, wiggling extrovert. Personalities and temperaments within a litter can range from extremely active to completely passive. Some puppies are ready to play with the world, others simply want to crawl up into your lap and be held. While you should never select a puppy that appears shy or listless because you feel sorry for him, do not hesitate to select a puppy that is calm and quiet, just as long as he is healthy.

Taking a puppy that appears sickly and needy will undoubtedly lead to heartache and expensive veterinary costs. Do not attempt to make up for what the breeder did not do in providing proper care and nutrition because it seldom works.

If at all possible, take the puppy you are attracted to into a different room of the kennel or house in which he was raised. The smells will remain the same for the puppy, so he should still feel secure. This will give you an opportunity to see how the puppy acts away from his littermates and a chance to inspect the puppy more closely.

Above all, the puppy should be clean. The skin should be pliable and the coat smooth and soft. The inside of a healthy puppy's ears will be pink and clean. Dark discharge or a bad odor could indicate ear mites, a sure sign of a lack of cleanliness and poor maintenance. A Boston puppy's breath should always smell sweet. The nose of a healthy puppy is cold and wet, and there should be no discharge of any kind. There should never be any malformation of the jaw, lips, or nostrils. Make sure there is no rupture of the navel.

The puppy's teeth must be clean and bright, and the eyes should be dark and clear. Runny eyes or eyes that appear red and irritated could be caused by a myriad of problems, none of which indicate a healthy puppy. Coughing and diarrhea are absolute danger signals.

A Boston puppy's movement should be free and easy, and he should never express any difficulty in moving about. Sound conformation can be determined even at eight or ten weeks of age.

The puppy's attitude tells you a great deal about his state of health. Puppies that are feeling "out of sorts" react very quickly and will usually find a warm littermate to snuggle with. They will prefer to stay that way even when the rest of the gang wants to play or go exploring.

MALE OR FEMALE?

The sex of a dog in many breeds is an important consideration and, of course, there are sex-related differences in the Boston that the prospective buyer should consider. In the end, however, the assets and liabilities of each sex do balance one another out, and the final choice in Bostons remains with the individual preference.

The male Boston makes just as loving and devoted a companion as the female. In some instances, he can perhaps be a bit more headstrong than an adolescent can. This could require a bit more patience

Choose the puppy that chooses you. The pup you pick should be excited to be with you and enjoy your attention and affection.

on the part of his owner. Here again, the owner's dedication to persistence in training will determine the final outcome.

The male dog of most breeds will have a natural instinct to lift his leg and urinate to "mark" his home territory. It seems confusing to many dog owners, but a male's marking of his home turf has nothing to do with whether or not the dog is housetrained. The two responses come from entirely different needs and must be dealt with in that manner. Some dogs are more difficult to train than others. Males that are used for breeding are even more prone to this response and are even harder to train.

Females have their semi-annual "heat" cycles once they have reached sexual maturity. These cycles usually occur for the first time at about nine or ten months of age. They last about 21 days and are accompanied by a bloody vaginal discharge for a part of that time. There are also "pants" that can be obtained from your pet shop that will help avoid her spotting the area in which she lives. It must be understood that the female has no control over this discharge, so it has nothing to do with training. Confinement of the female in heat is especially important to prevent unwanted attention from male dogs because she may become pregnant.

Choosing a male or female is a matter of personal preference—either one will make a good pet.

Make sure every member of your family is ready, willing, and able to take on the responsibility of raising a Boston Terrier puppy.

The spaying of the female and neutering of the male can eliminate problems. Unless a Boston is purchased expressly for breeding or showing from a breeder capable of making this judgment, your pet should be sexually altered.

It should be understood, however, that spaying and neutering are not reversible procedures. Spayed females and neutered males are not allowed to be shown in the conformation shows of most countries, nor will altered animals ever be able to be used for breeding.

SELECTING A SHOW-PROSPECT PUPPY

If you and your family are considering a show career for your puppy, we strongly advise putting yourself in the hands of an established breeder who has earned a reputation for breeding winning show dogs. He or she is most capable of anticipating what one might expect a young puppy of a certain line to develop into when he reaches maturity.

Any predictions a breeder is apt to make are based upon his or her experience with past litters that produced winning show dogs. It should be obvious that the more successful a breeder has been in

If you are interested in showing your dog, the breeder should be able to help you select a potential champion in the litter.

producing winning Bostons through the years, the broader their basis of comparison will be. "Quality begets quality" is an old stockman's adage that certainly applies in this instance.

The most any responsible breeder will say about an eight-week-old puppy is that he has "show potential." If you are serious about showing your Boston, most breeders strongly suggest waiting until a puppy is at least four or five months old before making any decisions.

The breed standard has a very detailed description of how a top-quality Boston should look and how he should move. Some things even the complete novice can determine, while other things take an expert's eye, and even they are educated guesses when evaluating puppies.

Many breeders believe the ideal time to select a show-prospect Boston Terrier puppy is eight weeks of age. A number of necessary characteristics can be determined at this age, and it is also a time when puppies may reflect, in miniature, what they will (or what their breeders *hope* they will) look like as adults.

Polly, bred by Hi-Society Boston Terriers, is a fine example of an excellent pet, as well as a winning show dog.

The show puppy should have a short-coupled, "cobby" little body with overall substance and good bone, and muscle development. The show Boston should never look overly refined, short-legged, or spindly. Evaluating movement, however, is something that requires an experienced opinion.

Some idea of the squareness of head and muzzle to skull proportions can be observed at this time. A short little muzzle is a must in the Boston puppy, as muzzle length often seems to increase as the youngster matures.

Ear and eye placement, as well as eye color and shape, can also be observed at this time. At eight weeks, ears may not be fully erect, and teething at four or five months can again cause even the best of ears to go up and down.

A good number of breeders like to see the teeth meet in a level or even slightly overshot bite. The reason for this is that the lower jaw grows longer than the upper jaw, and if undershot at eight weeks of age, the adult Boston may be grossly undershot as an adult.

Needless to say, you want the Boston show-prospect puppy to be healthy and outgoing, as well as mentally and physically sound. Regardless of what the future holds for your puppy, these characteristics are essential.

Color and markings are what they will always be at this age, and the Boston Terrier standard describes them well. Understand though, as important as color and markings are in this breed, they are not the standard's only requirements.

Even if a Boston Terrier puppy has aesthetic shortcomings, this would in no way interfere with his being a wonderful companion. At the same time, however, these faults could be serious drawbacks in the show ring. Many of these faults are such that a beginner in the breed might hardly notice. This is why employing the assistance of a good breeder is so important. Still, the prospective buyer should be at least generally aware of what the Boston Terrier show puppy should look like and know what faults would bar him from being a winner in the show ring.

The complete AKC standard of the Boston Terrier appears in this book and there are also a number of other books available that can assist the newcomer in learning more about the Boston. The more you know about the history and development of the breed, the better equipped you will be to see the differences that distinguish the show dog from the pet. However, the three most basic elements that really define a show-prospect puppy are type, balance, and temperament.

Type

Type includes the characteristics that differentiate the particular breed from all others. Paramount among these features, of course, is the Boston's distinctive head, with his sweet and inquisitive expression. The Boston Terrier's color and markings are also an especially important part of the breed's essence.

Balance

Balance is the manner in which all the desirable characteristics fit together. For instance, the Boston puppy's back is short and strong, and balance connects his two ends in such a manner that the youngster moves with ease.

Temperament

The correct Boston temperament combines all the wonderful characteristics that make him such a beloved companion. In the show ring, the Boston is a happy and determined performer—a dog that moves about with a casual air and love of life.

PUPPY OR ADULT?

For the person anticipating a show career for their Boston or for

It is important that puppies have time to play with their littermates in order to learn how to interact with other dogs later in life.

someone hoping to become a breeder, the purchase of a young adult provides greater certainty with respect to quality. Even those who simply want a companion can consider the adult dog.

In some instances, breeders will have males or females they no longer wish to use for breeding or have developed some show ring flaw that diminishes their chances for a successful show career. Also, on occasion, a Boston is returned to the breeder because the owner moves or is no longer able to keep a dog. Bostons of this kind could make a wonderful companion for someone, and acquiring an adult dog eliminates the many problems raising a puppy involves. Bostons are dogs that transfer well to the home, provided they are given the affection and attention they need.

Elderly people often prefer an adult dog, particularly one that is housetrained. The adult dog is easier to manage and requires less supervision and damage control. Adult Bostons are seldom chewers and usually more than ready to adapt to household rules.

However, there are other things to consider. Adult dogs have usually developed behaviors that may or may not fit into your routine. If an adult Boston has never been housetrained or has never been exposed to small children, it will take a very concentrated effort on the part of the new owner to compensate for these shortcomings.

Children are also inclined to be more active and vocal than the average adult is, and this could intimidate the dog as well. Properly introduced and supervised, however, the relationship between a Boston and a child will usually develop quickly and beautifully.

We strongly advise taking an adult Boston on a trial basis to see if the dog will adapt to the new owner's lifestyle and environment. Most often it works, but on rare occasions a prospective owner decides that training his or her dog from puppyhood is worth the time and effort required.

Important documents

The purchase of any purebred dog entitles you to three very important documents: a health record that includes a list of inoculations, a copy of the dog's pedigree, and a registration certificate.

Health and Inoculation Records

You will find that most Boston breeders have initiated the

A pedigree ensures that all of your puppy's ancestors were purebred Boston Terriers.

necessary, preliminary inoculation series for their puppies by the time they are eight weeks of age. These inoculations temporarily protect the puppies against hepatitis, leptospirosis, distemper, and canine parvovirus. Permanent inoculations will follow at a prescribed time. Since breeders and veterinarians follow different approaches to inoculations, it is important that the health record you obtain for your puppy accurately lists which shots have been given and when. In this way, the veterinarian you choose will be able to continue with the appropriate inoculation series as needed. In most cases, rabies inoculations are not given until a puppy is four months of age or older.

Pedigree

The pedigree is your Boston's family tree. The breeder must supply you with a copy of this document authenticating your puppy's ancestry back to at least the third generation. All purebred dogs have pedigrees. The pedigree in itself does not mean that your puppy is of show quality; it simply means that every one of his ancestors were, in fact, registered Boston Terriers.

Unscrupulous puppy dealers often try to imply that a pedigree indicates that all dogs having one are of championship caliber. This is not true. Again, a pedigree simply tells you that all of the dog's ancestors are purebred.

Registration Certificate

A registration certificate is the canine world's birth certificate. This certificate is issued by a country's governing kennel club. When the ownership of your Boston is transferred from the breeder's name to yours, the transaction is entered on this certificate and, once mailed to the appropriate kennel club, permanently recorded in their computerized files.

Keep all of your dog's documents in a safe place, as you will need them when you visit your veterinarian or should you ever wish to breed or show your Boston. Keep the name, address, and phone number of the breeder from whom you purchased your dog in a separate place as well. Should you ever lose any of these important documents, you will then be able to contact the breeder regarding obtaining duplicates.

Diet Sheet

When you bring your Boston puppy home for the first time, he should be a happy, healthy little extrovert. This is due in a good part to the care and feeding he received from the breeder. Every breeder we know has his or her own particular way of feeding. Most breeders give the new owner a written record that details the amount and kind of food a puppy has been receiving. Follow these recommendations to the letter, at least for the first month or two after the puppy comes to live with you.

The diet sheet should indicate both the kinds of food and the number of times a day your Boston puppy is accustomed to being fed. The kinds of vitamin supplementation the puppy has been receiving, if any, are also important. Following the prescribed procedure will reduce the chance of upset stomach and loose stools.

Usually, a breeder's diet sheet projects the increases and changes in food that will be necessary as your puppy grows from week to week. If the sheet does not include this information, ask the breeder for suggestions regarding increases and the eventual changeover to adult food.

Your breeder should provide you with a diet sheet that will indicate the type of food your puppy has been eating—follow this for the first few weeks to avoid stomach upsets.

In the unlikely event you are not supplied with a diet sheet by the breeder and are unable to get one, your veterinarian will be able to advise you in this respect. There are countless foods now being manufactured expressly to meet the nutritional needs of puppies and growing dogs. A trip down the pet aisle at your supermarket will prove just how many choices there are. Two important tips to remember: read labels carefully for content, and when dealing with established, reliable manufacturers, you are more likely to get what you pay for.

Health Guarantee

Any reputable breeder is more than willing to supply a written agreement that the purchase of your Boston is contingent upon his passing a veterinarian's examination. Ideally, you will be able to arrange an appointment with your chosen veterinarian right after you have picked up your puppy from the breeder and before you take the puppy home. If this is not possible, you should not delay this procedure any longer than 24 hours from the time the puppy leaves the breeder's home.

Socialize your puppy with different people, places, and things. A well-socialized dog will get along with anybody.

TEMPERAMENT AND SOCIALIZATION

Temperament is both hereditary and learned. Poor treatment and lack of proper socialization can ruin inherited good temperament. A Boston puppy that comes from shy or nervous stock is a poor risk to his owner in any capacity. A shy puppy would certainly not make a pleasant companion or winning show dog. An unstable Boston should never be bred. Therefore, it is critical that you obtain a happy puppy from a breeder who is determined to produce good temperaments and has taken all the necessary steps to provide the early socialization necessary.

Taking your puppy to a "puppy kindergarten" class is one of the best things you can do for him. There he will learn how to obey basic training commands, as well as how to interact with other dogs and people.

If you are fortunate enough to have children in the household or living nearby, your socialization task will be assisted considerably. Bostons raised with well-supervised children are usually very well behaved and socialized. The two seem to understand each other. In some way, known only to the puppies and children themselves, they give each other the confidence to face the trying ordeal of growing up.

The children in your own household are not the only children with whom your puppy can spend time—the more the merrier! Every child (or adult, for that matter) that enters your household should be introduced to your Boston. If trustworthy neighborhood children live nearby, have them come in and spend time with your puppy under adult supervision.

The children must understand, however, that puppies are babies and cannot endure rough handling, nor can they play for hours on

A puppy kindergarten class will introduce your Boston to basic obedience, as well as aid in the socialization process.

Your puppy should go everywhere with you—the more places he goes, the better socialized he will become.

end without rest periods. It is also important to teach young children the proper way to pick up and hold a Boston puppy. Children tend to pick puppies up by their front legs, which is not the proper way. Puppies should be picked up by supporting the rear and hindquarters with one hand and placing the other hand under the puppy's chest.

Weather permitting, your puppy should go everywhere with you—to the post office, the park, shopping malls, wherever. Be prepared to create a stir wherever you go because the very reason that attracted you to the first Boston you met applies to other people as well. Everyone will want to pet your little cherub and there is nothing in the world better for him.

Remember to never leave your Boston alone in a car during hot or even warm weather. Temperatures inside a closed car can soar in just a few minutes, and this could cause the death of your dog. Bostons are especially sensitive to heat. Leaving windows down does little to help and could lead to your dog attempting to escape through the open window or even providing an opportunity for someone to steal him.

If your Boston has a show career in his future, you will have to teach him other things in addition to just being handled. All show dogs, regardless of breed, must learn to have their mouth inspected by the judge. The judge must also be able to check the teeth. Males must be accustomed to having their testicles touched, as the dog show judge must determine that all male dogs are complete. This means there are two normal-sized testicles in the scrotum. These inspections must begin in puppyhood and be done on a regular and continuing basis.

THE ADOLESCENT BOSTON TERRIER

Boston puppies go through growth periods in spurts, where parts of the anatomy seem to develop independently of each other. One day your puppy will have a short and firm back, while the next day it will appear to sag, and the day after that it may look like a camel's hump. This is actually very normal. Eventually your Boston will almost always revert back to what gave him promise as a puppy.

Food needs change during this growth period. Think of Boston puppies as individualistic as children and act accordingly. The amount of food you give your Boston Terrier should be adjusted to how much he will consume at each meal and how that amount relates to optimum weight. Healthy Boston. Terriers normally have excellent appetites and some are willing to eat far more than they need to stay fit. You must be extremely careful not to let your dog get too fat.

A young Boston Terrier needs his owner to provide him with the guidance and discipline he needs to get along with his family.

Some Bostons can give you a forlorn look that says they are starving, regardless of how much food you give them. However, excess weight for Bostons can be lethal. If the entire meal is eaten quickly, add a small amount to the next feeding and continue to do so as the need increases. This method will ensure that you're giving your puppy enough food, but you must also pay close attention to your dog's appearance.

At eight weeks of age, a Boston puppy is eating four meals a day. By the time he is six months old, the puppy can do well on two meals a day, with perhaps a midday snack. If a puppy does not eat the food offered, he is either not hungry or not well. A healthy Boston will always eat when he is hungry. If you suspect the dog is not well, a trip to the veterinarian is in order.

This adolescent period is a particularly important one as it is the time your Boston must learn all the household and social rules by which he will live for the rest of his life. Your patience and commitment during this time will not only produce a respected canine good citizen, but will forge a bond between the two of you that will grow and ripen into a wonderful relationship.

CARING for Your Boston Terrier

FEEDING AND NUTRITION

Following the diet sheet provided by the breeder from whom you obtain your Boston puppy is the best way to make sure the puppy is obtaining the right amount and the correct type of food for his age. Do your best not to change the puppy's diet and you will be less apt to run into and diarrhea and digestive problems. Diarrhea is very serious in young puppies. Puppies with diarrhea can dehydrate rapidly, causing severe problems and even death.

If it is necessary to change your Boston puppy's diet for any reason, it should be done gradually over a period of several meals and a few days. Begin by adding a tablespoon or two of the new food and gradually increase the amount until the meal consists entirely of the new product.

At about six months of age, the Boston puppy can do well on three meals a day—morning, noon, and night. By the time your Boston is 10 to 12 months old, you can reduce feedings to once or

Consult your breeder or veterinarian about the proper diet for your Boston Terrier puppy.

twice a day. If you are feeding just one meal, it can be given either in the morning or evening. It is really a matter of choice on your part. There are two important things to remember: feed the main meal or meals at the same time every day, and make sure what you feed is nutritionally complete.

The single meal can be supplemented by a morning or nighttime snack of hard dog biscuits made especially for medium or small dogs. These biscuits are particularly good for a Boston's teeth and gums.

Balanced Diets

In order for a canine diet to qualify as "complete and balanced" in the US, it must meet standards set by the Subcommittee on Canine Nutrition of the National Research Council of the National Academy of Sciences. Most commercial foods manufactured for dogs meet these standards and prove this by listing the ingredients contained in the food on every package or can. The ingredients are listed in descending order with the main ingredient listed first.

Fed with any regularity at all, refined sugars can quickly cause your Boston to become obese and will defmitely create tooth decay. Candy stores do not exist in nature and canine teeth are not

Fresh, clean water should be offered to your dog several times a day, especially after playing or exercising.

Make sure you choose a good-quality food that is nutritious and appropriate for your dog's age and energy level.

genetically disposed to handling sugars. Do not feed your Boston Terrier candy or sweets, and avoid products that contain sugar to any high degree.

Fresh water and a properly prepared, balanced diet containing the essential nutrients in correct proportions are all a healthy Boston Terrier needs to be offered. Dog food is available canned, dry, semi-moist, "scientifically fortified," and "all-natural." A visit to your local supermarket or pet store will reveal how vast an array from which you will have to select.

All dogs, from toy to giant sized, are meat-eating animals, and the basis for the diet they are fed should be in animal protein. The product can be canned or dried, but check to make sure that the major ingredient (appearing first on the list) is, in fact, animal protein. But meat is not the only ingredient in a well-balanced canine diet, they also need carbohydrates and the minerals and nutrients present in vegetables.

Through centuries of domestication, we have made our dogs entirely dependent upon us for their well-being. Therefore, we are responsible for duplicating the food balance that the wild dog finds in nature. The domesticated dog's diet must include some protein, carbohydrates, fats, roughage, and small amounts of essential minerals and vitamins.

Finding commercially prepared diets that, according to the labels, contain all the necessary nutrients in the proper balance will not present a problem. It is important to understand that these commercially prepared foods contain a high concentration of the nutrients your Boston requires. While many Boston breeders recommend some vitamin supplementation for healthy coat and increased stamina, especially for show dogs, pregnant bitches, or growing puppies, it is important that discretion be used.

Over Supplementation

A great deal of controversy exists today regarding the orthopedic problems that afflict many breeds. Some claim these problems are entirely hereditary, but many others feel they can be exacerbated by overuse of mineral and vitamin supplements for puppies. Over-supplementation is now looked upon by some breeders as a major contributor to many skeletal abnormalities found in the purebred dogs of the day. In giving vitamin supplementation, one should *never* exceed the prescribed amount. No vitamin, however, is a substitute for a nutritious, balanced diet.

There is a growing trend among breeders to cook their dogs' food from scratch, combining their special mixture of vegetables and animal protein. In doing so, they eliminate the preservatives from their dogs' diets that are found in many commercially prepared foods. It is important to discuss this feeding method with your veterinarian so that you are sure to include all the necessary nutrients your dog requires.

Pregnant and lactating bitches do require supplementation of some kind, but again, it is not a case of "if a little is good, a lot would be better." Extreme caution is advised in this case, and the use of these supplements is best discussed with the breeder from whom you purchased your Boston or your veterinarian.

Table scraps should be given only as part of the dog's meal and never from the table. A Boston that becomes accustomed to being hand-fed from the table can become a real pest at mealtime very quickly. Also, dinner guests may find the woeful and pleading stare of your Boston is less than appealing when dinner is being served.

If you give your Boston Terrier treats, do so in moderation and make sure they do not upset his regular diet.

Dogs do not care if food looks like a hot dog or a piece of cheese, so you do not need to purchase foods that are manufactured to look like these foods. Truly nutritious dog foods are seldom manufactured to look like food that appeals to humans. Dogs only care about how food smells and tastes. It is highly doubtful that you will be eating your dog's food, so do not waste your money on these "looks just like" products.

Special Diets

There are many commercially prepared diets for dogs with special dietary needs. The overweight, underweight, or geriatric dog can have his nutritional needs met, as can puppies and growing dogs. The calorie content of these foods is adjusted accordingly. With the correct amount of the right foods and the proper amount of exercise, your Boston should stay in top shape. Again, common sense must prevail. Too many calories and too little exercise will increase weight. Increasing the amount of exercise and reducing the number of calories will reduce weight.

On occasion, a young Boston going through the teething period will become a poor eater. The concerned owner's first response is to tempt the dog by hand-feeding special treats and foods that the

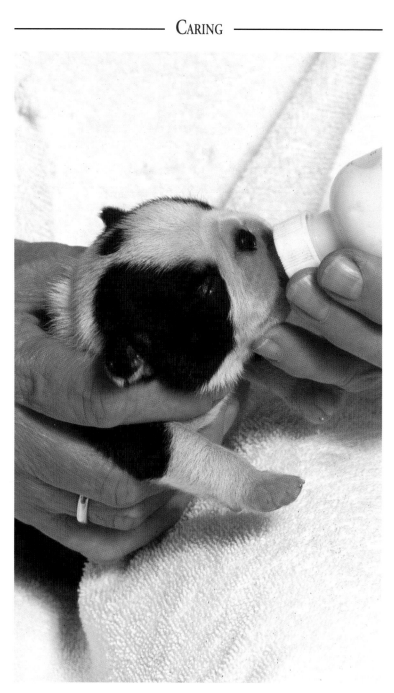

It is essential that your Boston puppy receive a healthy diet to get a good start in life.

problem eater seems to prefer. This practice only adds to the problem. Once the dog learns to play the waiting game, he will turn up his nose at anything other than his favorite food, knowing full well that what he *wants* to eat will eventually arrive.

Unlike humans, dogs have no suicidal tendencies. A healthy dog will not starve himself to death. He may not eat enough to keep him in the shape we find ideal and attractive, but he will definitely eat enough to maintain himself. If your Boston is not eating properly and appears to be too thin, it is probably best to consult your veterinarian.

SPECIAL NEEDS OF THE BOSTON TERRIER

Exercise

Exercise is important to the well-being of your Boston Terrier. It is an area that is too often neglected by Boston owners. This does not mean you must become a marathon jogger or mountain climber in order to accommodate your dog. However, a good brisk walk around a city block in the cool of the morning or after sunset can do nothing but improve your Boston's health and constitution.

If there are young children or other dogs or cats in your household, your Boston could already be getting enough exercise. Even at that, the Boston is always ready for a romp or a game. Slow, steady exercise keeps the heart rate healthy and extends your dog's life. If your Boston is doing all of this with you at his side, you are increasing the chances that the two of you will enjoy each other's company for many years to come.

Regular exercise is important to the well-being of your Boston Terrier.

Toys and Chewing

Although Boston Terriers are not notorious chewers, any young puppy can be very destructive during his teething period. The Boston puppy is able to find things that have yet to be lost and feels everything he finds should be stored in his tummy.

"Puppy proofing" your home is a must. Your Boston will be ingenious in getting into things he shouldn't, so you have to keep ahead of what your puppy might get himself into.

Provide toys that will keep the puppy busy and involved, and eliminate his need for eating your needlepoint pillow or the legs off your table. Just be sure to provide things that are hard to chew up. The original Nylabone®, or one of many rawhide products, is ideal.

Never give your puppy old shoes or discarded clothing to play with. Dogs can see no difference between a beat-up old sneaker you have given them and your brand new running shoes. Once you've worn shoes or clothing, they all smell *exactly* alike to your Boston—age and cost of the item notwithstanding.

Socialization

The Boston is, by nature, a happy, carefree dog and takes most situations in stride. It is important, however, to accommodate the

Chew toys like Nylabones® can help keep your belongings safe and your teething puppy's jaws occupied.

The Boston Terrier's short coat does little to protect him from cold weather, so keep him warm when outside for an extended period of time.

breed's natural instincts by making sure your dog is accustomed to everyday events of all kinds. Traffic, strange noises, loud or hyperactive children, and strange animals can be very intimidating to a dog of any breed that has never been exposed to them before. Gently and gradually introduce your puppy to as many strange situations as you possibly can.

Make it a practice to take your Boston with you whenever practical. The breed is a real crowd-pleaser, and you will find that your dog will savor all the attention he gets.

Heat and Cold

We cannot stress too heavily the danger in allowing your Boston Terrier to be exposed to high temperatures. As previously detailed, a Boston should never be allowed to remain in an automobile during hot weather, even for a few moments. Allowing this to happen is extremely dangerous. Nor should you permit your Boston to have any kind of extended heavy exercise during the heat of the day.

If your Boston spends time outdoors during the hot months, it is critical to provide a shaded area for the dog to retire to at all times. There should also be fresh, cool water available. If you are ever in doubt as to whether or not the outdoor temperature is too high for your Boston, it is best to assume that it is and keep your dog indoors.

The Boston is not equipped to cope with extremely low temperatures either. The breed's short, thin coat does little to protect from cold or wet weather. If your Boston is accompanying you on a short, brisk, winter walk, chances are he will be just fine, unless temperatures are sub-zero. If you plan on allowing your dog to be outdoors for an extended period of time when the temperatures are very low, consider investing in a coat for your dog. Some of these coats are also water repellent, but make sure your Boston is thoroughly dry when he comes back into your home.

BATHING AND GROOMING

The Boston does not have a long coat, but this does not mean the breed needs no grooming. Regular attendance to this matter assists

Daily brushing can help keep your Boston's coat shiny and healthy looking.

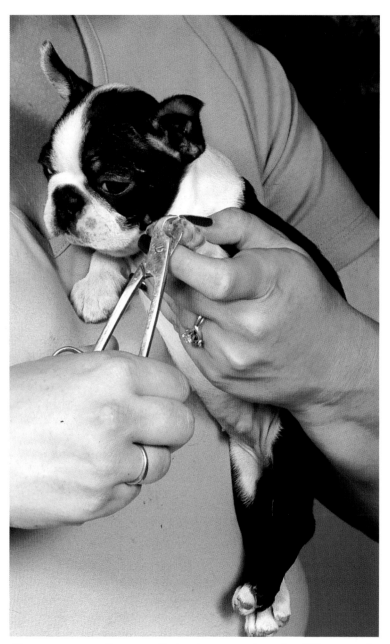

If you accustom your Boston to nail trimming at an early age, he will become used to the process as he matures.

both your Boston's health and appearance. Your puppy should become accustomed to standing quietly on a grooming table for his weekly "once-over." A stiff bristle brush applied with the lay of the hair will whisk away what little debris the Boston's coat holds, and a soft towel will restore the coat's shine.

Brushing should always be done in the same direction as the hair grows. You should begin at the dog's head, brushing toward the tail and down the sides and legs. This procedure will loosen the dead hair and brush it off the dog. This is the time to check the skin thoroughly for any abrasions or external parasites.

Removing the face whiskers is optional. Some owners feel long whiskers detract from the Boston's expression. Should you decide to do so, it is best to use curved, blunt-edged scissors to avoid damage to the dog's eyes.

Be aware that your Boston's eyes are prominent and can be prone to injury. Do not allow your dog to hang his head out of the window of your moving car. Flying debris can cause serious damage to the dog's eyes.

Nail Trimming

You will soon need to accustom your Boston to having his nails trimmed and feet inspected as part of his grooming routine. The Boston's dark nails make it difficult to see the blood vessel running through the center of the nail and into the quick, which grows close to the end of the nail and contains very sensitive nerve endings. If the nail is allowed to grow too long, it will be impossible to cut it back to a proper length without cutting into the quick. This causes severe pain to the dog and can also result in a great deal of bleeding that can be difficult to stop.

The nails of a Boston that spends most of his time indoors or on grass when outdoors can grow long very quickly. Do not allow the nails to become overgrown and then expect to cut them back easily. If your Boston is getting plenty of exercise on cement or rough, hard pavement, the nails may keep sufficiently worn down. Otherwise, the nails can grow long rapidly. They must then be carefully trimmed back with canine nail clippers, an electric nail grinder (also called a drummel), or a coarse file made expressly for that purpose.

Many owners use the electric or battery-operated nail grinder because it is easy to control and helps avoid cutting into the quick. Use of the electric grinder requires introducing your puppy to it at

Author Bob Candland uses a nail grinder to keep the toenails of his Boston Terrier neat and trim.

an early age. The instrument makes a whining sound not unlike a dentist's drill. The noise combined with the vibration of the sanding head on the nail itself can take some getting used to, but most dogs eventually accept it as one of life's trials.

Should the quick be nipped in the trimming process, there are many blood-clotting products available at pet shops that will almost immediately stem the flow of blood. It is wise to have one of these products on hand in case there is a nail trimming accident or the dog tears a nail on his own.

Always inspect your dog's feet for cracked pads and check between the toes for splinters and thorns. Pay particular attention to any swollen or tender areas. In many sections of the country, there is a weed called the foxtail that releases a small, barbed, hook-like object carrying the plant's seed. This hook easily finds its way into a Boston's foot or between his toes and very quickly works its way deep into the dog's flesh. This will quickly cause soreness and infection. These barbs should be removed by your veterinarian before a serious problem results.

Bathing

If brushing is done regularly, bathing will seldom be necessary

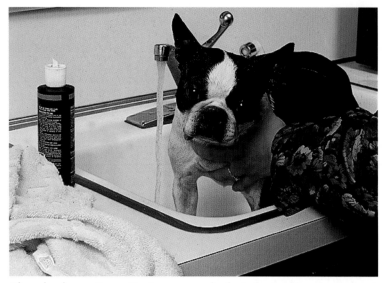

If you brush your Boston Terrier on a regular basis, he should need a bath only occasionally.

unless your Boston finds his way into something that leaves his coat with a disagreeable odor or that stains his white markings. Even then, there are many products, both dry and liquid, available at your local pet store that eliminate odors, clean the white hair, and leave the coat shiny and clean.

Use a shampoo made especially for dogs when you bathe your Boston. Place cotton in the ear canal to prevent water from entering this delicate area. Soak the dog with a shower hose and lather the coat twice. Rinse at least twice because soap residue, if allowed to remain in the coat, can cause dry skin and irritation.

Always towel-dry after the bath and keep your Boston indoors until completely dry. This applies in both summer and winter. Allowing your freshly bathed Boston out in the yard, even though it is warm outdoors, just might create the need for another bath. It is a dog's natural instinct to roll in the grass immediately after he has been bathed.

HOUSETRAINING and Training Your Boston Terrier

There is no breed of dog that cannot be trained. Some breeds appear to respond more slowly than others, but more often than not, this may be due to the trainer not being "breed specific" in his or her approach to the training than it is to the dog's inability to learn. The ease of training a dog of any breed greatly depends upon just how much a dog relies upon his master's approval. The Boston wants to please his owner and is a relatively easy breed to train.

The key to having a well-trained Boston is to start with play training when he is a very young puppy. While it may be difficult to remind ourselves that our wonderful Bostons trace back to the wolf, doing so will help in understanding our dogs. The wolf mother plays with her cubs, and part of that play results in teaching the cubs what they may and may not do. The Boston puppy, like his wolf-cub ancestor, does best when he thinks he is having fun and has decided on his own to participate. Do not allow your cute little Boston puppy to do something that you would not want him to do as an adult.

Every puppy can benefit from basic training, because it allows him to live in the house as part of the family.

A puppy's biting your hands or feet, refusing to give up a toy, or jumping on you or on furniture may appear cute and funny. Allowing a puppy to do this encourages the behavior, and he will continue to do this into adulthood. That will be far from cute and funny and extremely difficult to stop.

It is very important in training a Boston that the dog is absolutely confident of his place in the "pack" of humans the dog lives with.

HOUSETRAINING

Without a doubt, the best way to housetrain a Boston Terrier is to use what most breeders refer to as the crate method. First-time dog owners are inclined to initially see using the crate method of housetraining as cruel, but most dogs actually feel safe there and treat the crate as their home. All dogs need a place of their own to retreat to, and you will find your Boston will be comfortable and happy in his crate in no time at all. The use of a crate reduces housetraining time to an absolute minimum and avoids keeping a puppy under constant stress by incessantly correcting him for making mistakes in the house.

The crate used for housetraining should only be large enough so that the puppy can stand up, lie down, and stretch out comfortably. These crates are available at most pet stores in a wide range of prices. The Nylabone® Fold Away Pet Carrier is a perfect crate to use for your Boston Terrier.

Begin feeding your puppy in the crate. Keep the door closed and latched while the puppy is eating. When the meal is finished, open the cage and carry the puppy outdoors to the spot where you want him to learn to eliminate. As you are doing so, you should consistently use the same words. Whether the words are "go out," "potty," or any other phrase you like makes no difference. The important point is that the puppy will learn where to eliminate and that certain words mean that something is expected.

In the event that you do not have outdoor access or will be away from home for long periods of time, begin housetraining by placing newspapers in an out-of-the-way corner that is easily accessible for the puppy. If you consistently take your puppy to the same spot, you will reinforce the habit of going there for that purpose.

It is important that you do not let the puppy loose after eating. Young puppies will eliminate almost immediately after eating or drinking. They will also be ready to relieve themselves when they

Carte training is the fastest and easiest way to housetrain your Boston Terrier.

Buy a crate that your dog can stand up in and move around in comfortably.

first wake up and after playing. You will quickly learn when this is about to take place if you keep a watchful eye on your puppy. A puppy usually circles and sniffs the floor just before he relieves himself. Do not give your puppy an opportunity to learn that he can eliminate in the house. Your housetraining chores will be reduced considerably if you avoid bad habits in the first place.

If you are not able to watch your puppy every minute, he should be in his crate with the door securely latched. Each time you put your puppy in the crate, give him a small treat of some kind. Throw the treat to the back of the crate and encourage the puppy to walk in on his own. When he does so, praise the puppy and perhaps hand him another piece of the treat through the wires of the cage.

Do not succumb to your puppy's complaints about being in his crate. The puppy must learn to stay in his crate and to do so without unnecessary complaining. A quick "no" command and a tap on the crate will usually get the puppy to understand that his theatrics will not result in liberation.

An important point to remember, however, is that a puppy of 8 to 12 weeks will not be able to contain himself for long periods of time. Puppies of that age must relieve themselves every few hours, except at night. Your schedule must be adjusted accordingly.

Also make sure that your puppy has relieved himself of both bowel and bladder the last thing at night, and do not dawdle when you wake up in the morning. Your first priority in the morning is to get the puppy outdoors. Just how early this ritual takes place will depend much more upon your puppy than upon you. If your Boston is like most others, there will be no doubt in your mind when he needs to be let out. You will also quickly learn to tell the difference between a "this is an emergency" complaint and "I just want out" grumbling. Do not test the young puppy's ability to contain himself. His vocal demand to be let out is confirmation that the housetraining lesson is being learned.

Should you find it necessary to be away from home all day, you will not be able to leave your puppy in a crate. On the other hand, do not make the mistake of allowing him to roam the house, or even a large room, at will. Confine the puppy to a small room or partitioned area and cover the floor with newspaper. Make this area large enough so that the puppy will not have to relieve himself next to his bed, food, or water bowl. You will soon find that the puppy

Your Boston Terrier will soon come to think of his crate as a cozy place to retreat and relax.

will be inclined to use one particular spot to perform his bowel and bladder functions. When you are home, you must take the puppy to this exact spot to eliminate at the appropriate time.

BASIC TRAINING

Early "puppy kindergarten," along with puppy play training, are vital if you plan to do obedience work of any kind. The AKC annually records a significant number of Boston Terriers that have achieved Obedience titles. There are several titles that can be earned. You can obtain the requirements for each by writing the AKC and requesting their free booklet titled, *Obedience Regulations.*

The Companion Dog (CD) title is the least difficult to obtain. This level deals with the basics in which every Boston should be schooled: sit, stay, down, and heeling on and off leash. One might compare the title to obtaining a Bachelor's degree.

The Companion Dog Excellent (CDX) title is the next-most difficult. This would be comparable to a Master's degree. This level requires the dog to perform many of the same exercises he did to obtain the CD title but on a more sophisticated level. It also includes jumping obstacles and retrieving.

Make sure your dog has plenty of time outside to eliminate, especially during the housetraining process.

Buy an adjustable collar that will grow with your puppy and let him get used to wearing it gradually.

The more advanced degrees build upon what had been required in the previous levels and add scenting exercises as well. The Utility Dog (UD) title would be like our having completed a Doctorate degree. Training the Boston Terrier is limited only to the extent of his owner's ability and patience.

Your emotional state and the environment in which you train are just as important to your dog's training as is his state of mind at the time. Never begin training when you are irritated, distressed, or preoccupied. Nor should you begin basic training in a place that interferes with you or your dog's concentration. At first, the two of you should work in a place where you can concentrate fully upon one another. Once the commands are understood and learned, you can begin testing your dog in public places.

Leash Training

It is never too early to accustom the Boston puppy to a collar and leash. It is your way of keeping your dog under control. It may not be necessary for the puppy or adult Boston to wear his collar and identification tags within the confines of your home, but no dog should ever leave home without a collar and the leash.

Leash training your Boston at an early age will make it easier to practice the basic obedience commands.

Begin getting your puppy accustomed to his collar by leaving it on for a few minutes at a time. Gradually extend the time you leave the collar on. Most Bostons become accustomed to their collar very quickly and forget they are even wearing one.

Once this is accomplished, attach a lightweight leash to the collar while you are playing with the puppy. Do not try to guide the puppy at first. The point here is to accustom the puppy to the feeling of having something attached to the collar.

Encourage your puppy to follow you as you move away. Should the puppy be reluctant to cooperate, coax him along with a treat of some kind. Hold the treat in front of the puppy's nose to encourage him to follow you. Just as soon as the puppy takes a few steps toward you, praise him enthusiastically and continue to do so as you move along.

Make the initial sessions very brief and enjoyable. Continue the lessons in your home or yard until the puppy is completely unconcerned about the fact that he is on a leash. With a treat in one hand and the leash in the other, you can begin to use both to guide the puppy in the direction you wish to go. Your walks can begin in front of the house and eventually extend down the street and around the block.

The Come Command

Another important lesson for the Boston puppy to learn is to come when called, so it is very important that the puppy learn his name as soon as possible. Constant repetition does the trick in teaching a puppy his name—use the name every time you talk to your puppy.

Learning to come on command could save your dog's life when the two of you venture out into the world. Come is the command that a dog must understand has to be obeyed without question. The dog should not associate that command with fear. Your dog's response to his name and the word "come" should always be associated with a pleasant experience, such as great praise and petting or a food treat.

Remember, training your Boston Terrier early on to avoid the establishment of bad habits is much easier than it is to correct these behaviors once they are set. Never give the come command unless you are sure your Boston puppy will come to you.

A young puppy is far more inclined to respond to learning the come command than an older dog because puppies are more dependent upon their owners. Use the command initially, when the puppy is already on his way to you, or give the command while walking or running away from the youngster. Clap your hands and sound very happy and excited about having the puppy join in on

Your dog should learn to come to you on command, not only for his safety, but for the safety of others as well.

this game. A very young Boston will normally want to stay as close to his owner as possible, especially in strange surroundings. When your puppy sees you move away, his natural inclination will be to get close to you. This is a perfect time to use the come command.

Later, as the puppy grows more independent, you may want to attach a long leash or rope to the puppy's collar to ensure the correct response. Do not chase or punish your puppy for not obeying the come command. Doing so in the initial stages of training makes the youngster associate the command with something to resist, and this will result in avoidance rather than the immediate positive response you desire. It is imperative that you praise your Boston puppy and give him a treat when he does come to you, even if he voluntarily delays his response for many minutes.

The Sit and Stay Commands

This sit and stay commands are just as important to your Boston's safety as the no command and learning to come when called. Even very young Bostons can learn the sit command quickly, especially if it appears to be a game and a food treat is involved.

The sit command is the foundation for all other training commands. These Bostons practice their sit perfectly.

The Boston-in-training should always be on a collar and leash for all his lessons. Puppies are certainly not beyond getting up and walking away when they have decided something across the yard is far more interesting than your lessons.

It is usually easy to teach a dog to sit. Start with a lot of treats that your dog really likes. Hold a treat over your Boston's head and say, "Sit." Most dogs will raise their head to look at the treat, which will cause them to sit. If your dog sits, praise him and

You can help your Boston Terrier learn the sit command by gently placing him into position and praising him when he does what you ask.

give him the treat. Keep repeating this until he gets it. You can also reinforce the command by saying "sit" and giving a treat any time your dog sits on his own. This will help him to equate the word "sit" with the action. Make your Boston stay in this position for increasing lengths of time. Begin with a few seconds and increase the time as lessons progress over the following weeks.

If your Boston attempts to get up or to lie down, he should be corrected by simply saying, "Sit!" in a firm voice, and by giving him a treat when he gets back into position.

Only when you decide your dog should get up should he be allowed to do so. However, do not test the young Boston puppy's patience to the limits. Remember that you are dealing with a baby and the attention span of any youngster is relatively short.

When you do decide the dog can get up, call his name, say, "Okay," and make a big fuss over him. Praise and a food treat are in order every time your Boston responds correctly.

Every session should end with praise and a fun game so that your dog associates training with positive rewards.

Once your Boston has mastered the sit lesson, you may start on the stay command. With your dog on leash and facing you, command him to sit and then take a step or two backward. If your dog attempts to get up to follow, firmly say, "sit, stay!" While you are saying this, raise your hand, palm toward the dog, and again command, "stay!"

Any attempt on your dog's part to get up must be corrected at once, returning him to the sit position and repeating, "stay!" Once your dog begins to understand what you want, you can gradually increase the distance you step back. With a long leash or even a clothesline attached to your dog's collar, start with a few steps and gradually increase the distance to several yards. Your Boston must eventually learn that the sit, stay command must be obeyed no matter how far away you are. Later, with advanced training, your dog will learn that the command is to be obeyed even when you move entirely out of sight.

Avoid calling the dog to you at first. This makes the dog overly anxious to get up and come to you. Until your Boston masters the sit lesson and is able to remain in the sit position for as long as you dictate, walk back to your dog and say, "okay," which is a signal that the command is over. Later, when your dog becomes more reliable in this respect, you can call him to you.

The sit/stay lesson can take considerable time and patience, especially with the Boston puppy whose attention span will be very short. It is best to keep the stay part of the lesson to a minimum until a Boston is at least five or six months old. Everything in a very young and dependent Boston puppy's makeup will urge him to follow you wherever you go. Forcing a very young puppy to operate against his natural instincts may bewilder him.

The Down Command

Once your Boston has mastered the sit and stay commands, you may begin work on the down command. Use the down command only when you want the dog to lie down completely. If you want your Boston to get off your sofa or to stop jumping up on people, use the off command. Do not interchange these two commands. Doing so will only confuse your dog, and evoking the right response will become next to impossible.

The down position is especially useful if you want your Boston to remain in a particular place for a long period of time. A Boston is far more inclined to stay put when he is lying down rather than when he is sitting. However, lying in the correct position may not be as appealing to your Boston as perhaps stretching out on his side

Hand signals in conjunction with verbal commands can be very useful when training your Boston Terrier.

or even on his back. Correct obedience performance dictates that your dog lie on his stomach with his front legs stretched out ahead.

Teaching your Boston to obey this command properly may take more time and patience than the previous lessons the two of you have undertaken. Some animal behaviorists believe that assuming the down position somehow represents submissiveness to the dog. However, once the down command has become a part of your Boston's repertoire, it seems to be more relaxing for the dog, and you will find that he seems less inclined to get up and wander off.

With your Boston sitting so that he is facing you, hold a treat in your right hand with the excess part of the leash in your left. Hold the treat under the dog's nose and slowly bring your hand down to the ground. Your dog will follow the treat with his head and neck. As he does, give the down command.

An alternative method of getting your Boston headed into the down position is to move around to the dog's right side and, as you draw his attention downward with your right hand, slide your left arm under the dog's front legs and gently slide them forward. In the case of a very small Boston puppy or a tall owner, you will undoubtedly have to be on your knees next to the youngster.

As your Boston's forelegs begin to slide out forward, keep moving the treat along the ground until the dog's whole body is lying flat while you continually repeat, "down." Once your dog has assumes the position you desire, give him the treat and a lot of praise. Continue assisting your Boston into the down position until he does so on his own. Be firm and be patient.

The Heel Command

The heel command teaches your Boston to walk on your left side with his shoulder next to your leg, no matter which direction you might go or how quickly you turn. Teaching your Boston to heel will not only make your daily walks far more enjoyable, it will make a far more tractable companion when the two of you are in crowded or confusing situations. An untrained Boston, even when on a leash, can be nuisance to control, particularly if you are carrying packages, opening doors, or maneuvering stairs or elevators. Your Boston will want to be with you wherever you go, so training him to walk along in the correct position is usually not much of a problem.

The down command can be especially practical if you want your Boston Terrier to stay in one place for a long period of time.

The heel command will teach your dog to walk nicely by your side without pulling ahead.

In the beginning, when you are training your Boston puppy to walk along on the leash, you should accustom the youngster to walking on your left side. The leash should cross your body from the dog's collar to your right. The excess portion of the leash will be folded into your right hand. Your left hand should hold a treat that your Boston really likes.

Make sure your dog has is attention on you, which can be assisted by letting him smell the treat. Give the "heel" command as you start walking. Always keep the leash slack as long as your dog maintains the proper position at your side.

If your dog begins to drift away, stop in your tracks, lure the dog back to the correct position with the treat, and give the "heel" command. At first walk a few steps, then stop, have your dog sit, and give him the treat and lots of praise. Increase the amount of time you walk, always stopping if your dog moves away from your side. Soon you will be able to phase out the treats and just use praise.

TRAINING CLASSES

There are actually few limits to what a patient, consistent Boston owner can teach his or her dog. With a lot of praise and food treats, the road to success will be much easier for the both of you.

For advanced obedience work beyond the basics, it is wise for the Boston owner to consider local professional assistance. Professional trainers have had long-standing experience in avoiding the pitfalls of obedience training and can help you to avoid them as well. The strange dogs and new people encountered at training classes are also particularly good for your Boston's socialization.

There are free-of-charge classes at many parks and recreation facilities, as well as formal and sometimes very expensive individual lessons with private trainers. There are also some obedience schools that will take your Boston and train him for you. However, unless your schedule provides no time at all to train your own dog, having someone else train the dog should only be used as a last resort. The rapport that develops between the dog and the owner who has trained his or her Boston to be a pleasant companion and good

A canine good citizen will be able to obey obedience commands and will be trustworthy around people.

canine citizen is very special—it is well worth the time and patience it requires to achieve.

BOSTON TERRIER VERSATILITY

Once your Boston has been taught his basic manners, there are countless ways that the two of you can participate in enjoyable events. The breed is very successful in conformation shows and has proven he can excel in obedience competition as well.

Canine Good Citizen Test

A good introduction to more advanced obedience training are the requirements for a Canine Good Citizen certificate. A dog that passes a ten-part test as designed by the American Kennel Club (AKC) earns this certificate. These tests include cleanliness and grooming, socialization, obeying simple commands, and general tractability. As the name implies, any dog capable of earning the certificate can only be a better friend and companion.

Therapy Dogs

Bostons can perform an extremely valuable service by visiting homes for the aged, orphanages, and hospitals. Bostons love people, and people of all ages love a Boston's sweet expression and inquisitive ways. It is amazing to see how kind and gentle Bostons are with small children and with people who are ill or feeble. It has been proven that these visits provide great therapeutic value to the patients.

The well-trained Boston can provide a whole world of activities for the owner. You are only limited by the amount of time you wish to invest in this remarkable breed.

BEHAVIOR and Canine Communication

S tudies of the human/animal bond point out the importance of the unique relationships that exist between people and their pets. Those of us who share our lives with pets understand the special part they play through companionship, service, and protection. For many, the pet/owner bond goes beyond simple companionship; pets are often considered members of the family. A leading pet food manufacturer recently conducted a nationwide survey of pet owners to gauge just how important pets were in their lives. Here's what they found:

• 76 percent allow their pets to sleep on their beds
• 78 percent think of their pets as their children
• 84 percent display photos of their pets, mostly in their homes
• 84 percent think that their pets react to their own emotions
• 100 percent talk to their pets
• 97 percent think that their pets understand what they're saying

Are you surprised?

Senior citizens show more concern for their own eating habits when they have the responsibility of feeding a dog. Seeing that their dogs are routinely exercised encourages the owners to think of schedules that otherwise may seem unimportant to senior citizens. The older owner may be arthritic and feeling poorly, but with responsibility for a dog, he or she has a reason to get up and get moving. It is a big plus if his or her dog is an attention-seeker that will demand such from his owner.

Over the last couple of decades, it has been shown that pets relieve the stress of those who lead busy lives. Owning a

Ashley and her Boston Terrier friend Fred can get along so well because of good training and socialization.

pet has been known to lessen the occurrence of heart attack and stroke.

Many single folks thrive on the companionship of their dogs. Lifestyles are very different from a long time ago, and today more individuals seek the single life. However, they receive fulfillment from owning dogs.

Most likely, the majority of dogs live in family environments. The companionship they provide is well worth the effort involved. Children in particular benefit from the opportunity to have a family dog. Dogs teach responsibility through the understanding of their care, feelings, and even respect for their life cycles. Frequently, those children who have not been exposed to dogs grow up afraid of them, which isn't good. Dogs sense timidity, and some will take advantage of the situation.

Today, more dogs are working as service dogs. Since the origination of the Seeing Eye Dogs years ago, many dogs are trained to aid the deaf. Also, dogs are trained to provide service for the handicapped and are able to perform many different tasks for their owners. Search and rescue dogs, with their handlers, are sent throughout the world to assist in the recovery of disaster victims. They are lifesavers. Some dogs become therapy dogs and are very popular with nursing homes, and hospitals. The inhabitants truly look forward to their visits.

Nationally, there is a Pet Awareness Week to educate students and others about the value and basic care of our pets. Many countries take an even greater interest in their pets than Americans do. In those countries, pets are allowed to accompany their owners into restaurants and shops, etc. In the US, this freedom is only available to our service dogs. Even so, people still think very highly of the human/animal bond.

SOCIALIZING AND TRAINING

Many prospective puppy buyers lack experience regarding the proper socialization and training needed to develop a desirable pet. In the first 18 months, training does take some work, but it is easier to start proper training before there is a problem that needs to be corrected.

The initial work begins with the breeder, who should start socializing the puppy at five to six weeks of age. Human socializing is critical up through 12 weeks of age and is likewise important

Your puppy is just a baby—you have to show him how to behave in your household.

during the following months. The litter should be left together during the first few weeks, but it is necessary to separate the pups by ten weeks of age. Leaving them together after that time will increase competition for litter dominance. If puppies are not socialized with people by 12 weeks of age, they will be timid in later life.

The eight- to ten-week age period can be a fearful time for puppies. They need to be handled very gently by children and adults. There should be no harsh discipline during this time. Starting at 14 weeks of age, the puppy begins the juvenile period, which ends when he reaches sexual maturity around 6 to 14 months of age. During the juvenile period, he needs to be introduced to strangers (adults, children, and other dogs) on the home property. At sexual maturity, he will begin to bark at strangers and become more protective. Males start to lift their legs to urinate, but you can inhibit this behavior by walking him on a leash away from trees, shrubs, fences, etc.

Puppy training classes are great places to socialize your puppy with other dogs and start his training. However, make sure he has all his vaccinations before taking him to meet other dogs.

Consistency is the key to reinforcing good behavior. If you are consistent in training, your puppy will always know what is expected of him.

Socialization and training are a crucial part of your dog's development and allow him to live as part of your household and family. In order for your dog to live harmoniously in your home, he should know the household rules. You should always be consistent; this way, your dog knows what is expected of him at all times. Even the most well-trained dog may exhibit problem behavior, often due to his natural instincts: for instance, some dogs are very vocal barkers, some dogs are born to dig, some dogs will run and chase anything that moves. It takes consistent work and patience, but if your dog knows the rules, you can curb problem behavior and help your dog to become part of the family.

SOLVING PROBLEMS

Barking
Barking can be a breed trait or a bad habit learned through the environment. It takes dedication to stop the barking. Overzealous barking can be a breed tendency. When barking presents a problem for you, try to stop it as soon as it begins.

If your dog has a barking problem, it is important first to discover why your dog is barking, and then deal with the situation accordingly.

If your dog is barking because of loneliness or boredom, a chew toy can help to keep him busy and quiet while you are gone.

To solve barking problems, you first have to determine the cause. Perhaps it gets your attention—the perfect reward. If you run and bring him inside when he barks, he learns that barking gets what he wants—you. He may be barking because he's protecting your property from perceived (or real) threats, there may be other dogs or children playing nearby, he may be playing, or perhaps he's afraid of something. Some dogs are just more vocal than others and will always be barky, no matter what you do. However, you can control the noise factor with prevention and training.

The best way to stop outside "attention" barking is to ignore him until he realizes barking is futile and he quiets down. If it is bothering the neighbors, bring him inside and crate him, letting him out only when he's quiet.

Yelling at your dog may seem like the thing to do when he's barking, but it's actually counterproductive. To him, your yelling sounds like barking, and when you yell, he will bark more. Yelling just proves to him that the perceived threat is real, or else why would the pack leader be barking too?

If your dog is easily stimulated by what is going on outside, make sure you draw the curtains so that he isn't distracted by every leaf that blows by. Do not yell or make a fuss when he does bark. After he barks once or twice, tell him to be quiet and give him praise and a treat when he stops. Soon he will learn that he gets rewards for being quiet, not barking.

If your dog is barking inside the house when he is alone, he might be suffering from separation anxiety. A dog that has separation anxiety is inconsolable when you leave the house, whining and barking, perhaps scratching at the door. He may also destroy things while you're gone.

In order to help control this problem, don't make a big fuss about saying hello and goodbye when you enter or leave the house. In fact, don't greet your barking dog at all until he has calmed down. Ignore him. When you pet him, you're just rewarding the behavior. Only pet him when he has stopped barking and after you've asked him to sit.

Be sure to crate him or confine him to a safe room when you are gone so that he doesn't get a chance to destroy anything. Put on the television or the radio so that he feels like he has company. Make sure he gets plenty of exercise and a chance to eliminate before you leave and give him plenty of chew toys to keep him occupied.

If your dog often barks his head off in the crate, try this: About 30 minutes before you leave, give him his Nyla-bone® or a Rhino® stuffed with peanut butter or cheese and then ignore him just as if you were already gone. Don't talk to him, don't say good-bye; just leave. (This also works if you don't leave your

Most dogs jump up because they are happy or excited, but with training, you can channel your puppy's exuberant energy into a more positive response.

dog in a crate). When you return, don't say hello or make a big deal about coming home; just walk right past the crate and ignore him for about five minutes. When he quiets down, take him directly outside to relieve himself. Don't take him out of the crate when he's barking. The rationale behind this is that if you acknowledge him the minute you get home, he'll anticipate your return and bark the entire time you're gone.

Another solution for barking inside is to pretend you're leaving as an exercise to get your dog used to your comings and goings. Place your dog in the crate, put on your coat, take your car keys and walk around the house for a few minutes, then let him out if he's quiet and praise him. Next, dress up again, then walk out the door for 30 seconds. Do it again for 2 minutes, then 5, 10, 20, and so on. If he's quiet when you return, praise him verbally. If he's barking, just ignore him until he calms down, even if only for a moment. Do this over several days to several weeks and he should get used to your leaving him.

Teach your dog to sit instead of jumping to greet people and try not to encourage jumping at all, even when playing.

Jumping Up

A dog that jumps up is a happy dog. Nevertheless, few guests appreciate dogs jumping on them.

Some trainers believe in allowing the puppy to jump up during his first few weeks. If you correct him too soon and at the wrong age, you may intimidate him and he could be timid around humans later in his life. However, there will come a time, probably around four months of age, that he needs to know when it is okay to jump and when he is to show good manners by sitting instead.

If your dog jumping up on you irritates you, then you

should discourage it from the beginning. Jumping can actually cause harm or injury, especially to a senior citizen or children.

How do you correct the problem? All family members need to participate in teaching the puppy to sit as soon as he starts to jump up. The sit must be practiced every time he does it. Don't forget to praise him for his good behavior. Let him know that he only gets petted if he sits first. If he gets up while being petted, stop petting him and tell him to sit again. Tell everyone in the household and anyone who visits not to touch your dog or give him any attention unless he earns it by sitting first.

If he is a really bad jumper, ask family members and friends to help. Keep dog treats by the door and ask your visitors to tell your dog to sit when they come over. Keep him on his leash to keep him under control and have your guests give him the treat when he sits nicely. With time and patience, he will soon be sitting to greet everyone. Remember, the entire family must take part. Each time you allow your dog to jump up you go back a step in training.

The Runaway

There is little excuse for a dog to run away, because dogs should never be off leash except when supervised in a fenced-in yard.

Many prospective owners want to purchase a female because they believe a male is inclined to roam. It is true that an intact male is inclined to roam, which is one of the reasons a male should be neutered. However, females will roam also, especially if they are in heat. Regardless, these dogs should never be given this opportunity.

The first thing to remember is not to discipline your dog when you finally catch him after an escape. The

Close supervision and a securely fenced yard will lessen your dog's opportunity to run away.

reasoning behind this is that it is quite possible there could be a repeat performance, and you don't want your dog to be afraid to come to you when you call him.

Always kneel down when trying to catch the runaway. Dogs are afraid of people standing over them. Also, it would be helpful to have a treat or a favorite toy to help entice him to your side. After that initial runaway experience, start practicing the recall with your dog.

Chewing

From 3 to 12 months of age, puppies chew on everything. Your shoes, your newspaper, your neighbor's fingers—anything he can get his teeth on. He's not doing it out of spite or boredom. Chewing is natural behavior, relieving tension and anxiety, and it's fun. Puppies also have to chew because their teeth and gums hurt while they are teething.

Stop your dog from chewing the wrong things by only allowing him to chew on his own toys. Never give him your old shoes, slippers, or socks—he won't be able to distinguish a new pair from an old one. Nylabone® products are great chew toys for both puppies and older dogs. Confining your dog to a crate whenever you can't keep an eye on him and puppy proofing your home will also help stop your dog from chewing on things he shouldn't. Remember, puppies *have* to chew. Even after their adult teeth come in, dogs chew to clean and massage their teeth and gums. Give them a safe alternative.

Biting, Nipping, and Mouthing

Biting, mouthing, and nipping are unacceptable behavior, even in young dogs. What may seem cute in a little pup is not going to be so cute when he is a 100-pound adult.

Remember that rough play, wrestling, and tug-of-war aggravate and even teach these unwanted behaviors. Teasing your pup and playing chasing games can also encourage nipping. Your pup has an innate response to hunt and hold on to things. A simple game of tug-of-war to you means a lot more to your pup than it does to you.

When your puppy nips or bites you, snatch your hand away and say, "No! Ouch!" Then stop playing with him and ignore him. If your puppy is really overexcited and won't calm down,

Chewing is a natural canine behavior, so be sure to provide your dog with plenty of safe chew toys.

put him in his crate. Your puppy must realize that you will only play with him and have fun with him if he plays nicely.

Also, be very careful when your puppy is playing with children. Kids can get just as overexcited as puppies do, and the games can get out of hand. Always supervise children and dogs when they are together and, if it gets too rough, institute a "time out" and confine both the puppy and the child before someone gets hurt. Only let them play if they can be calm around each other.

Aggression

Any act of aggression on your puppy's part should be considered serious. Remember, your cute growling puppy may be an intimidating growling dog one day. If you socialize your puppy properly, you should not have an aggression problem. Remember, no rough play or wrestling, and no praise for nipping.

Your puppy may become possessive over various things: his territory, his owners, or his food, or he might show aggression when he is scared. This is where training comes in handy. Your puppy must realize from the beginning that where he lives is *your* house and he is living by *your* rules. A pup that thinks he has to protect everything, including you, will be aggressive, and for good reason—he's got a big job. But if you teach him from the beginning that you are the leader, you shouldn't have a problem.

Your dog should let you take things away from him or approach his food bowl. He should not growl or snap That bowl is *your* bowl, and that food is *your* food—you should be able to approach anytime you'd like. If you have this problem, approach the bowl with a treat, this will condition your dog to view you approaching the bowl as something pleasant. Keep doing it often and always praise him when he gives things up, and then make sure you give it back to him as his reward for sharing.

Counter Surfers and Trash Spreaders

Dogs jump up on tables because it often rewards them with a tasty dinner, and the scents in your trash cans are just too hard to resist for most dogs. This behavior is best dealt with by preventing it in the first place. Don't give your dog human food or, if you're a softie, put the morsel in his dish and don't let him see that it has come from the counter or the table.

Good management will help to control this behavior. Avoid the counter problem by confining the dog and keeping him out of the kitchen or dining area when you can't supervise him. The simplest way to avoid a "trash hound" is to move the trash out of your dog's reach or buy a trash can with a cover that locks.

If your dog does get into the food he shouldn't, only correct him if you catch him in the act. Just like housetraining, your dog won't associate the punishment with the food he stole an hour ago or the trash he knocked over this morning. Just chalk it up to experience and practice good management in the future.

Good management and dogproofing your house will help prevent your dog from eating something he shouldn't.

Some dogs dig to release pent-up energy, so make sure your Boston gets plenty of exercise to avoid replanting your garden.

Digging

Dogs dig because they're programmed to dig. Terriers, for example, "go to ground," meaning that they find prey in holes in the earth. To them, digging is fun and natural. Some dogs dig because they want to get out of a confined area, and others dig to release pent-up energy. They also dig to get away from the heat, so make sure your dog has plenty of drinking water and shady shelter when he's outside.

If you've got a particularly stubborn digger, you can fence off the places where you don't want him to dig and allocate a place in your yard where the dog will be allowed to dig. Let him know that it's okay for him to dig there by bringing him over to the spot and placing a toy or treat on the ground. Later, put it slightly under the dirt and maybe help him dig. When you catch him digging in the wrong place, bring him to his digging place. Show your approval by praising his digging in the right spot.

Stool Eating

Puppies do eat their own stool and even the stool of other

animals. This is called coprophagia. It's not the most pleasant of things, but it's a normal habit, and most pups get over it as they grow older. The best solution is to keep your yard really clean and take away the opportunity for your dog to eat anything he shouldn't. However, talk to your veterinarian and after you have determined that it's not a medical condition or a health problem, ask him to prescribe a medicine that makes the poop taste terrible. You can also spray his poop with Bitter Apple or vinegar—or both. If your pup gets into your cat's litter box, consider moving the box to another location. Sometimes changing a dog's diet and feeding him twice a day will stop coprophagia.

Submissive Wetting

Some puppies urinate when they're particularly excited, like when you come home. Most pups that do this will grow out of the behavior in time. However, submissive dogs aren't urinating when the owner comes home because they are excited—they pee because the leader has engaged them with some form of dominance, such as looking at them (eye contact), petting on the head and neck, or

Building your dog's confidence with basic training will help you to control many problem behaviors.

Praise your dog for his successes and help him to feel more secure in his good behavior.

bending over them. The submissive wolf in the wild would immediately roll over and wet itself when challenged even slightly by a dominant member of the pack. Because you are the dominant member of your pack, the submissive wetter is just doing what seems natural.

The best way to treat this problem is by confining the dog to an area where he can't greet you or your guests right away—he has to get used to new stimuli gradually. Like with separation anxiety, make your comings and goings as low key as possible so the dog doesn't get overly excited.

Use treats instead of praise for successful greetings (no wetting). Manage the greeting of guests in a controlled area where wetting is okay (outside), and have the dog on a leash and in a sit so that he can't charge the guests in his excitement. Praise, praise, praise for each success and have patience. The gentler you are to a dog that has this problem, the faster he will get over it.

Car Sickness

Car sickness usually starts when your dog is a puppy, but if you train him to enjoy riding in a car, you may avoid it. There are several

Make sure you feed your puppy several hours before you get in the card to avoid carsickness.

causes of car sickness; the most common are motion of the car, excitement, and anxiety.

Introduce your dog to the car gradually, while he's still young. Don't feed him just before or just after the ride. To accustom him to the car, put him in it and praise him calmly, then take him out and praise him again, without going anywhere. Give him a treat if he'll take it. Follow this routine a few times until he begins to relax.

Now, put him back in the car and start the engine. After a minute, turn it off, take the puppy out and play with him. Do this a few

Patience, persistence, and practice are essential keys to training your dog and creating a bond that will last a lifetime.

times, then take him for a short ride, perhaps halfway down the street. Again, play with him afterward. Do this training over an extended period of time when you're not in a rush.

When the dog becomes calm in the car, take him to the park or someplace that's fun for him. If he only rides in the car to get a vaccination or to be dropped off at the boarding kennel, it could remember the car as a negative experience.

Remember to make riding in the car an enjoyable experience. If possible, put him in a crate; he'll be more comfortable there than sitting between a couple of rowdy kids. There are even seat belts made for dogs. Make sure the car is not too hot, and never, ever leave your dog in the car with the windows closed, not even for two minutes. Besides being against the law, your dog could die of heatstroke.

Excessive Fear

The terrified pup begs for holding and coddling, trembling in the corner or under the bed at certain sounds or in certain situations, looking around for any kind of comfort. The problem with soothing a terrified dog is that it rewards the behavior and rewards exaggerated fear. After all, there's nothing for the pup to be afraid of in a thunderstorm, is there? Your puppy has no reason to fear the new plant in the corner of your living room or the vacuum cleaner. But he shivers, whines, and cries anyway, and if you coddle him, he'll believe that there is indeed something to be afraid of and he'll remember that. He'll think—If all it takes to get a bunch of hugs and lots of petting is to look terrified, that's not such a hard bill to fill. It is best to ignore your pup when he's afraid for no good reason. If you must acknowledge his terror, just give him a little pat on the head, tell him it's going to be okay, then go about your business. Give him a treat when he's afraid or put the treats on the object he is afraid of so that he associates it with positive things.

SPORT of Purebred Dogs

Welcome to the exciting and sometimes frustrating sport of dogs. No doubt you are trying to learn more about dogs, or you wouldn't be deep into this book. This section covers the basics that may entice you, further your knowledge, and help you to understand the dog world.

Dog showing has been a very popular sport for a long time and has been taken quite seriously by some. Others only enjoy it as a hobby.

The Kennel Club in England was formed in 1859, the American Kennel Club was established in 1884, and the Canadian Kennel Club was formed in 1888. The purpose of these clubs was to register purebred dogs and maintain their stud books. In the beginning, the concept of registering dogs was not readily accepted. However, more than 36 million dogs have been enrolled in the AKC Stud Book since its inception in 1888. Presently, the kennel clubs not only register dogs, but they also adopt and enforce rules and regulations governing dog shows, obedience trials, and field trials. Over the years they have fostered and encouraged interest in the health and welfare of the purebred dog. They routinely donate funds to veterinary research for study on genetic disorders.

Below are the addresses of the kennel clubs in the United States, Great Britain, and Canada.

American Kennel Club
260 Madison Avenue
New York, NY 10016
or 5580 Centerview Drive,
Raleigh, NC 27606

The Kennel Club
1 Clarges Street
Picadilly, London, WIY 8AB, England

The Canadian Kennel Club
89 Skyway Avenue
Etobicoke, Ontario, Canada M9W 6R4

Successful showing requires dedication, training, and preparation, but many find it extremely rewarding and lots of fun.

Today there are numerous activities that are enjoyable for both the dog and the handler. Some of the activities include conformation showing, obedience competition, tracking, agility, the Canine Good Citizen® Certificate, and a wide range of instinct tests that vary from breed to breed. Where you start depends upon your goals, which early on may not be readily apparent.

PUPPY KINDERGARTEN

Every puppy will benefit from this class. PKT is the foundation for all future dog activities from conformation to "couch potatoes." Pet owners should make an effort to attend, even if they never expect to show their dogs. The class is designed for puppies about three months of age with graduation at approximately five months of age. All the puppies will be in the same age group, and, even though some may be a little unruly, there should not be any real problem. This class will teach the puppy some beginning obedience. As in all obedience classes, the owner learns how to train his own dog. The PKT class gives the puppy the opportunity to interact with other puppies in the same age group and exposes him to strangers, which is very important. Some dogs grow up with

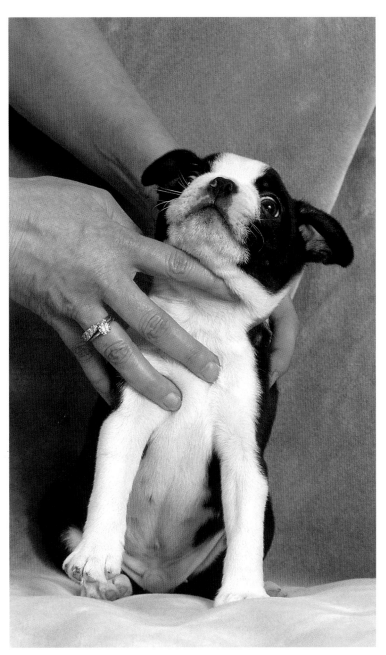

Every puppy can benefit from a puppy kindergarten class.

behavior problems, one of them being fear of strangers. As you can see, there can be much to gain from this class.

There are some basic obedience exercises that every dog should learn. Some of these can be started with puppy kindergarten.

CONFORMATION

Conformation showing is the oldest dog show sport. This type of showing is based on the dog's appearance—that is his structure, movement, and attitude. When considering this type of showing, you need to be aware of your breed's standard and be able to evaluate your dog compared to that standard. The breeder of your puppy or other experienced breeders would be good sources for such an evaluation. Puppies can go through many changes over a period of time. Many puppies start out as promising hopefuls and then after maturing may be disappointing as show candidates. Even so, this should not deter them from being excellent pets.

Conformation training classes are usually offered by the local kennel or obedience clubs. These are excellent places for training puppies. The puppy should be able to walk on a lead before entering such a class. Proper ring procedure and technique for posing (stacking) the dog will be demonstrated, as well as gaiting the dog. Generally, certain patterns are used in the ring, such as the triangle or the "L." Conformation class, like the PKT class, will give your

Champion dogs are carefully bred—this litter is the offspring of Am. Can. Ch. Zuran's Daisy May 'N Hi Society and Am. Can. Ch. Abacab's Encore Grand Finale.

youngster the opportunity to socialize with different breeds of dog and humans, too.

It takes some time to learn the routine of conformation showing. Usually, one starts at the puppy matches that may be AKC sanctioned or fun matches. These matches are generally for puppies from 2 or 3 months to a year old, and there may be classes for the adult over the age of 12 months. Similar to point shows, the classes are divided by sex, and after completion of the classes in that breed or variety, the class winners compete for Best of Breed or Variety. The winner goes on to compete in the Group, and the Group winners compete for Best in Match. No championship points are awarded for match wins.

In conformation, your Boston Terrier will be judged on how closely he conforms to the breed standard.

A few matches can be great training for puppies, even if there is no intention to go on showing. Matches enable the puppy to meet new people and be handled by a stranger—the judge. It also offers a change of environment, which broadens the horizon for both dog and handler. Matches and other dog activities boost the confidence of the handler, especially the younger handlers.

The AKC championship is built on a point system, which is different from Great Britain. To become an AKC Champion of Record, the dog must earn 15 points. The number of points earned each time depends upon the number of dogs in competition. The number of points available at each show depends upon the breed, its sex, and the location of the show. The US is divided into ten AKC zones. Each zone has its own set of points. The purpose of the zones is to try to equalize the points available from breed to breed and area to area. The AKC adjusts the point scale annually.

The number of points that can be won at a show are between one and five. Three-, four- and five-point wins are considered majors.

Not only does the dog need 15 points won under 3 different judges, but those points must include 2 majors under 2 different judges. Canada also works on a point system, but majors are not required.

Males always show before bitches. The classes available to those seeking points are: Puppy (which may be divided into 6 to 9 months and 9 to 12 months); 12 to 18 months; Novice; Bred-by-Exhibitor; American-bred; and Open. The class winners of the same sex of each breed or variety compete against each other for Winners Dog and Winners Bitch. A Reserve Winners Dog and Reserve Winners Bitch are also awarded but do not carry any points unless the original win is disallowed by AKC. The Winners Dog and Bitch compete with the Specials (those dogs that have attained championship) for Best of Breed or Variety, Best of Winners, and Best of Opposite Sex. It is possible to pick up an extra point or even a major if the points are higher for the defeated winner than those of Best of Winners. The latter would get the higher total from the defeated winner.

At an all-breed show, each Best of Breed or Variety winner will go on to his respective Group and then the Group winners will compete against each other for Best in Show. There are seven Groups: Sporting, Hounds, Working, Terriers, Toys, Non-Sporting, and Herding. Obviously, there are no Groups at specialty shows (those shows that have only one breed or a show such as the American Spaniel Club's Flushing Spaniel Show, which is for all flushing spaniel breeds).

Earning a championship in England is somewhat different since they do not have a point system. Challenge Certificates are awarded if the judge feels the dog deserves it, regardless of the number of dogs in competition. A dog must earn 3 Challenge Certificates under 3 different judges, with at least 1 of these Certificates being won after the age of 12 months. Competition is very strong and entries may be higher than they are in the US. The Kennel Club's Challenge Certificates are only available at championship shows.

In England, The Kennel Club regulations require that certain dogs, Border Collies and gundog breeds, qualify in a working capacity (i.e., obedience or field trials) before becoming a Full Champion. If they do not qualify in the working aspect, then they are designated a show champion, which is equivalent to the AKC's Champion of Record. A gundog may be granted the title of Field Trial Champion (FTCh.) if he passes all the tests in the field, but would also have to qualify in conformation before becoming a Full Champion. A Border Collie that earns the title of Obedience Champion (ObCh.) must also qualify in the conformation ring before becoming a champion.

The US doesn't have a designation for Full Champion but does award for Dual and Triple Champions. The Dual Champion must be a Champion of Record, and either Champion Tracker, Herding Champion, Obedience Trial Champion, or Field Champion. Any dog that has been awarded the titles of Champion of Record, and any two of the following: Champion Tracker, Herding Champion, Obedience Trial Champion or Field Champion, may be designated as a Triple Champion.

The shows in England seem to put more emphasis on breeder judges than those in the US. There is much competition within the breeds. Therefore, the quality of the individual breeds should be very good. In the US, there tend to be more "all-around judges," (those that judge multiple breeds) and use the breeder judges at the

Even if your Boston Terrier never enters a show, he can only benefit from the training that you provide him.

specialty shows. Breeder judges are more familiar with their own breed as they are actively breeding that breed or did so at one time. Americans emphasize Group and Best in Show wins and promote them accordingly.

The shows in England can be very large and extend over several days, with the Groups being scheduled on different days. Though multi-day shows are not common in the US, there are cluster shows in which several different clubs will use the same show site over consecutive days.

The Westminster Kennel Club is the most prestigious dog show in the US, although the entry is limited to 2500. In recent years, entry has been limited to champions. This show is more formal than the majority of the shows, with the judges wearing formal attire and the handlers fashionably dressed. In most instances, the quality of the dogs is superb. After all, it is a show of champions. It is a good show to study the AKC registered breeds and is by far the most exciting—especially since it is televised. WKC is one of the few shows in this country that is still benched. This means the dog must be in his benched area during the show hours, except when he is being groomed, is in the ring, or being exercised.

Typically, the handlers are very particular about their appearances. They are careful not to wear something that will detract from their dogs, but will perhaps enhance them. American ring procedure is quite formal compared to that of other countries. There is a certain etiquette expected between the judge and exhibitor and among the other exhibitors. Of course, it is not always the case, but the judge is supposed to be polite, not engaging in small talk, or acknowledging how well he knows the handler. There is a more informal and relaxed atmosphere at the shows in other countries. For instance, the dress code is more casual. The US is very handler-oriented in many of the breeds.

In England, Crufts is The Kennel Club's show and is most assuredly the largest dog show in the world. It's been known to have an entry of nearly 20,000, and the show lasts four days. Entry is only gained by qualifying through winning in specified classes at another championship show. Westminster is strictly conformation, but Crufts exhibitors and spectators enjoy not only conformation, but also obedience, agility, and a multitude of exhibitions, as well. Obedience was admitted in 1957 and agility in 1983.

You should be prepared with plenty of supplies when you go to a dog show, as well as a few familiar toys to make your dog feel comfortable.

If you are handling your own dog, please give some consideration to your apparel. The dress code at matches is more informal than at the point shows. However, you should wear something a little more appropriate than beach attire or ragged jeans and bare feet. If you check out the handlers and see what is presently fashionable, you'll catch on. Men usually dress with a shirt and tie and a nice sports coat. Whether you are male or female, you will want to wear comfortable clothes and shoes. You need to be able to run with your dog, and you certainly don't want to take a chance of falling and hurting yourself. Women usually wear a dress or two-piece outfit, preferably with pockets to carry bait, brush, etc. Ladies, think about where your dress will be if you need to kneel on the floor, and also think about running. Does it allow freedom to do so?

You need to take along the following items to the show with your dog: crate; ex pen (if you use one); extra bedding; water pail and water; all required grooming equipment; table; chair for you; bait for dog and lunch for you and friends; and, last but not least, clean-up materials, such as plastic bags, paper towels, and perhaps a damp towel—just in case. Don't forget your entry confirmation and directions to the show.

If you are showing in obedience, you may want to wear pants. Many of our top obedience handlers wear pants that are color-coordinated with their dogs. The philosophy is that imperfections in the black dog will be less obvious next to your black pants.

Whether you are showing in conformation, Junior Showmanship, or obedience, you need to watch the clock and be sure you are not late. It is customary to pick up your conformation armband a few minutes before the start of the class. They will not wait for you, and if you are on the show grounds and not in the ring, you will upset everyone. It's a little more complicated picking up your obedience armband if you show later in the class. If you have not picked it up and they get to your number, you may not be allowed to show. It's best to pick up your armband early, but be aware that you may show earlier than expected if other handlers don't pick up. Customarily, all conflicts should be discussed with the judge prior to the start of the class.

Junior Showmanship

The Junior Showmanship Class is a wonderful way to build self-confidence, even if there are no aspirations of staying with the dog showing later in life. Frequently, Junior Showmanship becomes the background of those who become successful exhibitors/handlers in the future. In some instances, it is taken very seriously, and success is measured in terms of wins. The Junior Handler is judged solely on his ability and skill in presenting his dog. The dog's conformation is not to be considered by the judge. Even so, the condition and grooming of the dog may be a reflection upon the handler.

Any Boston that competes in dog shows will have to get used to extensive grooming.

Participating in junior handling classes can teach children respect and love for animals. Boston Terriers Babs and Martha make friends with Callie and Jenna Plouffe.

Usually, the matches and point shows include different classes. The Junior Handler's dog may be entered in a breed or obedience class and even shown by another person in that class. Junior Showmanship classes are usually divided by age and perhaps sex. The age is determined by the handler's age on the day of the show. The classes are:

Novice Junior for those at least 10 and under 14 years of age, who at the time of entry closing have not won 3 first places in a Novice Class at a licensed or member show.

Novice Senior for those at least 14 and under 18 years of age, who at the time of entry closing have not won 3 first places in a Novice Class at a licensed or member show.

Open Junior for those at least 10 and under 14 years of age, who at the time of entry closing have won at least 3 first places in a Novice Junior Showmanship Class at a licensed or member show with competition present.

Open Senior for those at least 14 and under 18 years of age, who at the time of entry closing have won at least 3 first places in a Novice Junior Showmanship Class at a licensed or member show with competition present.

Junior Handlers must include their AKC Junior Handler number on each show entry. This needs to be obtained from the AKC.

CANINE GOOD CITIZEN®

The AKC sponsors a program to encourage dog owners to train their dogs. Local clubs perform the pass/fail tests, and dogs that pass are awarded a Canine Good Citizen® Certificate. Proof of vaccination is required at the time of participation. The test includes:

1. Accepting a friendly stranger.
2. Sitting politely for petting.
3. Appearance and grooming.
4. Walking on a loose leash.
5. Walking through a crowd.
6. Sit and down on command/staying in place.
7. Coming when called.
8. Reaction to another dog.
9. Reactions to distractions.
10. Supervised separation.

These well-behaved dogs are from Hi-Stiles Kennels and were bred by Shirley Stiles. Almost every one has earned their championship.

OBEDIENCE

Obedience is necessary, without a doubt, but it can also become a wonderful hobby or even an obsession. Obedience classes and competition can provide wonderful companionship, not only with your dog but also with your classmates or fellow competitors. It is always gratifying to discuss your dog's problems with others who have had similar experiences. The AKC acknowledged obedience around 1936, and it has changed tremendously, even though many of the exercises are basically the same. Today, obedience competition is just that—very competitive. Even so, it is possible for every obedience exhibitor to come home a winner (by earning qualifying scores), even though he/she may not earn a placement in the class.

Most of the obedience titles are awarded after earning three qualifying scores (legs) in the appropriate class under three different judges. These classes offer a perfect score of 200, which is extremely rare. Each of the class exercises has its own point value. A leg is earned after receiving a score of at least 170 and at least 50 percent of the points available in each exercise. The titles are:

Companion Dog—CD

This is called the Novice Class and the exercises are:

1. Heel on leash and figure 8	40 points
2. Stand for examination	30 points
3. Heel free	40 points
4. Recall	30 points
5. Long sit—one minute	30 points
6. Long down—three minutes	30 points
Maximum total score	200 points

Companion Dog Excellent—CDX

This is the Open Class and the exercises are:

1. Heel off leash and figure 8	40 points
2. Drop on recall	30 points
3. Retrieve on flat	20 points
4. Retrieve over high jump	30 points
5. Broad jump	20 points
6. Long sit—three minutes (out of sight)	30 points
7. Long down—five minutes (out of sight)	30 points
Maximum total score	200 points

Utility Dog—UD

The Utility Class exercises are:

1. Signal exercise	40 points
2. Scent discrimination-Article 1	30 points
3. Scent discrimination-Article 2	30 points
4. Directed retrieve	30 points
5. Moving stand and examination	30 points
6. Directed jumping	40 points
Maximum total score	200 points

After achieving the UD title, you may feel inclined to go after the UDX and/or OTCh. The UDX (Utility Dog Excellent) title went into effect in January 1994. It is not easily attained. The title requires qualifying simultaneously ten times in Open B and Utility B, but not necessarily at consecutive shows.

The OTCh. (Obedience Trial Champion) is awarded after the dog has earned his UD and then goes on to earn 100 championship points, a first place in Utility, a first place in Open, and another first place in either class. The placements must be won under three different judges at all-breed obedience trials. The points are determined by the number of dogs competing in the Open B and Utility B classes. The OTCh. title precedes the dog's name.

Obedience matches (AKC-sanctioned, fun, and show-and-go) are often available. Usually, they are sponsored by the local obedience clubs. When preparing an obedience dog for a title, you will find matches very helpful. Fun matches and show-and-go matches are more lenient in allowing you to make corrections in the ring. This type of training is usually very necessary for the Open and Utility classes. AKC-sanctioned obedience matches do not allow corrections in the ring since they must abide by the AKC obedience regulations booklet. If you are interested in showing in obedience, you should contact the AKC for a copy of *Obedience Regulations.*

TRACKING

Tracking is officially classified as obedience. There are three tracking titles available: Tracking Dog (TD), Tracking Dog Excellent (TDX), and Variable Surface Tracking (VST). If all three tracking titles are obtained, then the dog officially becomes a CT (Champion Tracker). The CT will go in front of the dog's name.

A TD may be earned anytime and does not have to follow the other obedience titles. There are many exhibitors that prefer tracking to obedience, and there are others who do both.

Tracking Dog—TD

A dog must be certified by an AKC tracking judge to perform in an AKC test. The AKC can provide the names of tracking judges in your area that you can contact for certification. Depending on where you live, you may have to travel a distance if there is no local tracking judge nearby. The certification track will be equivalent

With proper training, the intelligent and versatile Boston Terrier can excel at almost anything he sets his mind to do.

to a regular AKC track. A regulation track must be 440 to 500 yards long, with at least two right-angle turns out in the open. The track will be aged 30 minutes to 2 hours. The handler has two starting flags at the beginning of the track to indicate the direction started. The dog works on a harness and 40-foot lead and must work at least 20 feet in front of the handler. An article (either a dark glove or wallet) will be dropped at the end of the track, and the dog must indicate it but not necessarily retrieve it.

People always ask what the dog tracks. Initially, the beginner on the short-aged track tracks the tracklayer. Eventually, the dog learns to track the disturbed vegetation and learns to differentiate between tracks. Getting started with tracking requires reading the AKC regulations and a good book on tracking, plus finding other tracking enthusiasts. Work on the buddy system. That is, lay tracks for each other so you can practice blind tracks. It is possible to train on your own, but if you are a beginner, it is a lot more entertaining

Competing in dog shows and other competitions should be fun for both the dog and the owner.

to track with a buddy. It's rewarding seeing the dog use his natural ability.

Tracking Dog Excellent—TDX

The TDX track is 800 to 1000 yards long and is aged 3 to 5 hours. There will be five to seven turns. An article is left at the starting flag, and three other articles must be indicated on the track. There is only one flag at the start, so it is a blind start. Approximately one and a half hours after the track is laid, two tracklayers will cross over the track at two different places to test the dog's ability to stay with the original track. There will be at least two obstacles on the track, such as a change of cover, fences, creeks, ditches, etc. The dog must have a TD before entering a TDX. There is no certification required for a TDX.

Variable Surface Tracking—VST

This test came into effect in September 1995. The dog must have a TD earned at least six months prior to entering this test. The track is 600 to 800 yards long and will have a minimum of 3 different surfaces. Vegetation will be included along with two areas devoid of vegetation, such as concrete, asphalt, gravel, sand, hard pan, or mulch. The areas devoid of vegetation shall comprise at least one-third to one-half of the track. The track is aged three to five hours. There will be four to eight turns and four numbered articles, including one leather, one plastic, one metal, and one fabric dropped on the track. There is one starting flag. The handler will work at least ten feet from the dog.

AGILITY

Agility was first introduced by John Varley at the Crufts Dog Show in England in February 1978, but Peter Meanwell, competitor and judge, actually developed the idea. It was officially recognized in the early 1980s. Agility is extremely popular in England and Canada and growing in popularity in the US. The AKC acknowledged agility in August 1994. Dogs must be at least 12 months of age to be entered. It is a fascinating sport that the dog, handler, and spectators enjoy to the utmost.

Agility is a spectator sport in which the dog performs off lead. The handler either runs with his dog or positions himself on the course. He then directs his dog with verbal and hand signals over a timed course, over or through a variety of obstacles, including a time out or pause. One of the main drawbacks to agility is finding

The energetic Boston Terrier enjoys participating in many dog sports—even just a game in yard makes the breed very happy.

Performance tests allow your dog to take his natural instincts and training into the show ring.

Treats, toys, and playtime can be great training motivators for your Boston Terrier.

a place to train. The obstacles take up a lot of space, and it is very time consuming to put up and take down courses.

The titles earned at AKC agility trials are Novice Agility Dog (NAD), Open Agility Dog (OAD), Agility Dog Excellent (ADX), and Master Agility Excellent (MAX). In order to acquire an agility title, a dog must earn a qualifying score in his respective class on three separate occasions under two different judges. The MAX will be awarded after earning ten qualifying scores in the Agility Excellent Class.

GENERAL INFORMATION

Obedience, tracking, and agility allow the purebred dog with an Indefinite Listing Privilege (ILP) number or a limited registration to be exhibited and earn titles. Application must be made to the AKC for an ILP number.

The American Kennel Club publishes *Events*, a monthly magazine that is part of the *Gazette*, their official journal for the sport of purebred dogs. The *Events* section lists upcoming shows and the secretary or superintendent for them. The majority of the conformation shows in the US are overseen by licensed superintendents. Generally, the entry closing date is approximately two-and-a-half weeks before the actual show. Point shows are fairly expensive, while the match shows cost about one-third of the point show entry fee. Match shows usually take entries the day of the show, but some are pre-entry. The best way to find match show information is through your local kennel club. Upon asking, the AKC can provide you with a list of superintendents, and you can write and ask to be put on their mailing lists.

Obedience trial and tracking test information is also available through the AKC. Frequently, these events are not superintended, but put on by the host club. Therefore, you would make the entry with the event's secretary.

There are numerous activities you can share with your dog. Regardless of what you do, it does take teamwork. Your dog can only benefit from your attention and training.

HEALTH CARE

Veterinary medicine has become far more sophisticated than what was available to our ancestors. This can be attributed to the increase in household pets and, consequently, the demand for better care for them. Also, human medicine has become far more complex. Today, diagnostic testing in veterinary medicine parallels human diagnostics. Because of better technology, we can expect our pets to live healthier lives, thereby increasing their life spans.

THE FIRST CHECKUP

You will want to take your new puppy/dog in for his first checkup within 48 to 72 hours after acquiring him. Many breeders strongly recommend this checkup and so do the humane shelters. A puppy/dog can appear healthy, but he may have a serious problem that is not apparent to the layman. Most pets have some type of a minor flaw that may never cause a real problem.

This first checkup is a good time to establish yourself with the veterinarian and to learn the office policy regarding their hours and how they handle emergencies. Usually, the breeder or another conscientious pet owner is a good reference for locating a capable veterinarian. You should be aware that not all vets give the same quality of service. You should not make your selection based on the least expensive clinic, as they may be shortchanging your pet. However, there is the possibility that it will eventually cost you more due to improper diagnosis, treatment, etc.

If you are selecting a new veterinarian, feel free to ask for a tour of the clinic. You should inquire about making an appointment for a tour, because all clinics are working clinics, and therefore, may not be available all day for sightseers. You may worry less if you see where your pet will be spending the day if he ever needs to be hospitalized.

THE PHYSICAL EXAM

Your veterinarian will check your pet's overall condition, which includes listening to the heart; checking the respiration; feeling the abdomen, muscles, and joints; checking the mouth, which includes gum color and signs of gum disease, along with plaque buildup;

Proper health care from the start of your Boston Terrier's life will ensure that he has a long and healthy future.

checking the ears for signs of an infection or ear mites; examining the eyes; and, last but not least, checking the condition of the skin and coat.

He should ask you questions regarding your pet's eating and elimination habits and invite you to relay your questions. It is a good idea to prepare a list so as not to forget anything. He should discuss the proper diet and the quantity to feed. If this differs from your breeder's recommendation, you should convey to him what the breeder's choice is and see if he approves. If he recommends changing the diet, this should be done over a few days so as not to cause a gastrointestinal upset.

It is customary to take in a fresh stool sample (just a small amount) to test for intestinal parasites. It must be fresh, preferably within 12 hours, because the eggs hatch quickly and after hatching will not be observed under the microscope. If your pet isn't obliging, the technician can usually take a sample in the clinic.

IMMUNIZATIONS

It is important that you take your puppy/dog's vaccination record with you on your first visit. In the case of a puppy, presumably the breeder has seen to the vaccinations up to the time you acquired custody. Veterinarians differ in their vaccination protocol. It is not unusual for your puppy to have received vaccinations for distemper, hepatitis, leptospirosis, parvovirus, and parainfluenza every two to three weeks from the age of five or six weeks. Usually, this is a combined injection and is typically called the DHLPP.

The DHLPP is given through at least 12 to 14 weeks of age, and it is customary to continue with another parvovirus vaccine at 16 to 18 weeks. You may wonder why so many immunizations are necessary. A puppy inherits antibodies in the womb from his mother, but no one knows for sure when these antibodies actually leave the puppy's body, although it is customarily accepted that distemper antibodies are gone by 12 weeks. Usually, parvovirus antibodies are gone by 16 to 18 weeks of age. However, it is possible for the maternal antibodies to be gone much earlier or even at a later age. Therefore, immunizations are started at an early age. The vaccine will not give immunity as long as there are maternal antibodies.

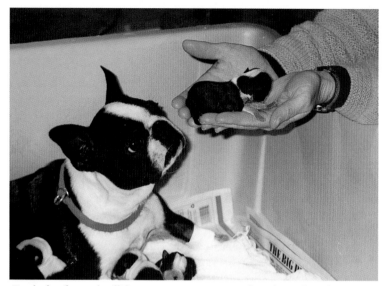

For the first few weeks of life, puppies receive immunity from disease from their mothers but need to start vaccinations as soon as possible.

The rabies vaccination is given at three or six months of age, depending on your local laws. A vaccine for bordetella (kennel cough) is advisable and can be given any time from the age of five weeks. The coronavirus is not commonly given unless there is a problem locally. The Lyme vaccine is necessary in endemic areas. Lyme disease has been reported in 47 states.

Distemper

Distemper is virtually an incurable disease. If the dog recovers, he is subject to severe nervous disorders. The virus attacks every tissue in the body and resembles a bad cold with a fever. It can cause a runny nose and eyes and gastrointestinal disorders, which casues a poor appetite, vomiting, and diarrhea. The virus is carried by raccoons, foxes, wolves, mink, and other dogs. Unvaccinated youngsters and senior citizens are very susceptible. This is still a common disease.

Hepatitis

Hepatitis is a virus that is most serious in very young dogs. It is spread by contact with an infected animal or its stool or urine. The virus affects the liver and kidneys and is characterized by high fever, depression, and lack of appetite. Recovered animals may be afflicted with chronic illnesses.

Leptospirosis
Leptospirosis is a bacterial disease transmitted by contact with the urine of an infected dog, rat, or other wildlife. It produces severe symptoms of fever, depression, jaundice, and internal bleeding and was fatal before the vaccine was developed. Recovered dogs can be carriers, and the disease can be transmitted from dogs to humans.

Parvovirus
Parvovirus was first noted in the late 1970s and is still a fatal disease. However, with proper vaccinations, early diagnosis, and prompt treatment, it is a manageable disease. It attacks the bone marrow and intestinal tract. The symptoms include depression, loss of appetite, vomiting, diarrhea, and collapse. Immediate medical attention is necessary in order to manage the disease.

Rabies
Rabies is shed in the saliva and is carried by raccoons, skunks, foxes, other dogs, and cats. It attacks nerve tissue, resulting in paralysis and death. Rabies can be transmitted to people and is virtually always fatal. This disease is reappearing in the suburbs.

Bordetella (Kennel Cough)
The symptoms of bordetella are coughing, sneezing, hacking, and retching,

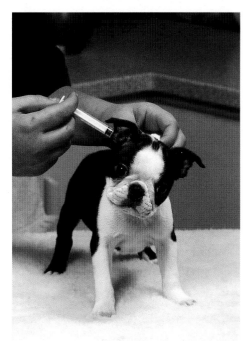

Your puppy's first exam will cover many general health issues, and the veterinarian should start him on his vaccination schedule.

Small puppies are very vulnerable and rely on you to take care of all their health needs.

accompanied by nasal discharge usually lasting from a few days to several weeks. There are several disease-producing organisms responsible for this disease. The present vaccines are helpful but do not protect for all the strains. It is usually not life threatening, but in some instances it can progress to a serious broncho-pneumonia. The disease is highly contagious. The vaccination should be given routinely for dogs that come into contact with other dogs, such as through boarding, training class, or visits to the groomer.

Coronavirus

Coronavirus is usually self-limiting and not a life-threatening disease. It was first noted in the late 1970s about a year before parvovirus. The virus produces a yellow/brown stool, and there may be depression, vomiting, and diarrhea.

Lyme Disease

Lyme disease was first diagnosed in the US in 1976 in Lyme, CT, in people who lived in close proximity to the deer tick. The disease is usually spread by these ticks, and symptoms may include acute lameness, fever, swelling of joints, and loss of appetite. Your veterinarian can advise you if you live in an endemic area.

Booster Shots

After your puppy has completed his puppy vaccinations, you will continue to booster the DHLPP once a year. It is customary to booster the rabies one year after the first vaccine and then, depending on where you live, the booster should be given every year or every three years, depending on your local laws. The Lyme and corona vaccines are boostered annually, and it is recommended that the bordetella be boostered every six to eight months.

ANNUAL VISIT

The annual checkup, which includes booster vaccinations, a check for intestinal parasites, and a test for heartworm, is extremely important. However, make sure to get this checkup from a qualified veterinarian, because more harm than good can come to your dog through improper vaccinations, possibly from inferior vaccines and/or the wrong schedule. It is also important for your veterinarian to know your dog, and this is especially true during middle age and through the geriatric years. Your older dog may require more than one physical a year. The annual physical is good preventive medicine. Through early diagnosis and subsequent treatment, your dog can maintain a longer and better quality of life.

INTESTINAL PARASITES

Hookworms

Hookworms are almost microscopic intestinal worms that can cause anemia and, therefore, serious problems, including death, in young puppies. Hookworms can be transmitted to humans through penetration of the skin. Puppies may be born with them.

Dogs can pick up parasites from other dogs, so make sure your Boston has all his shots before taking him out to make friends.

Roundworms

Roundworms are spaghetti-like worms that can cause a potbellied appearance and dull coat, along with more severe symptoms such as vomiting, diarrhea, and coughing. Puppies acquire these while in the mother's uterus and through lactation. Both hookworms and roundworms may be acquired through ingestion.

Whipworms

Whipworms have a three-month life cycle and are not acquired through the dam. They cause intermittent diarrhea, usually with mucus. Whipworms are possibly the most difficult worm to eradicate. Their eggs are very resistant to most environmental factors and can last for years until the proper conditions enable them to mature. Whipworms are seldom seen in the stool.

Intestinal parasites are more prevalent in some areas than others. Climate, soil, and contamination are big factors contributing to the incidence of intestinal parasites. Eggs are passed in the stool, lie on the ground, and then become infective in a certain number of days. Each of the above worms has a different life cycle. Your dog's best chance of becoming and remaining worm-free is to always keep

Good nutrition is an important part of your Boston Terrier's healthy lifestyle.

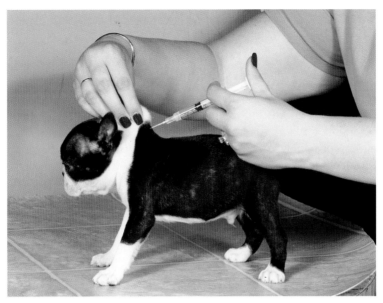

Regular booster shots and vet visits can keep your Boston healthy from puppyhood to adulthood.

your yard clean and free of the dog's fecal matter. A fenced-in yard keeps stray dogs out, which is certainly helpful.

Having a fecal examination done on your dog twice a year, or more often if there is a problem, is recommended. If your dog has a positive fecal sample, he will be given the appropriate medication and you will be asked to bring back another stool sample in a certain period of time (depending on the type of worm); then he will be rewormed. This process goes on until he has at least two negative samples. Different types of worm require different medications. You will be wasting your money and doing your dog an injustice by buying over-the-counter medication without first consulting your veterinarian.

OTHER INTERNAL PARASITES

Coccidiosis and Giardiasis

Coccidiosis and giardiasis, which are protozoal infections, usually affect pups, especially in places where large numbers of puppies are brought together. Older dogs may harbor these infections but do not show signs unless they are stressed. Symptoms include diarrhea, weight loss, and lack of appetite. These infections are not always apparent in the fecal examination.

Tapeworms

Seldom apparent on fecal floatation, tapeworms frequently show up as rice-like segments around the dog's anus and the base of the tail. Tapeworms are long, flat, and ribbon-like, sometimes several feet in length, and made up of many segments about five-eighths of an inch long. There are two common causes of tapeworm found in the dog. First, the larval form of the flea tapeworm parasite could mature in an intermediate host, the flea, before it can become infective. Your dog acquires this by ingesting the flea through licking and chewing. Secondly, rabbits, rodents, and certain large game animals serve as intermediate hosts for other species of tapeworm. If your dog eats one of these infected hosts, he can acquire tapeworms.

HEARTWORM DISEASE

Heartworm is a worm that resides in the heart and adjacent blood vessels of the lung that produces microfilaria, which circulate in the bloodstream. It is possible for a dog to be infected with any number of these worms, which are 6 to 14 inches long. It is a life-threatening disease, expensive to treat, and easily prevented. Depending on where you live, your veterinarian may recommend a preventive year-round and either an annual or semiannual blood test. The most common preventive is given once a month.

EXTERNAL PARASITES

Fleas

Fleas are not only the dog's worst enemies, but they are also enemies to the owner's pocketbook. Likely, the majority of our dogs are allergic to the bite of a flea, and in many cases, it only takes one fleabite to require treatment. The protein in the flea's saliva is the culprit. Allergic dogs have a reaction, which usually results in a "hot spot." More than likely, such a reaction will involve a trip to the veterinarian for treatment. Fortunately, today there are several good products available to help prevent fleas and eliminate them when there is an outbreak.

If there is a flea infestation, no one product is going to correct the problem. Not only will the dog require treatment, but the environment also will. In general, flea collars are not always very effective, although there is an "egg" collar now available that will kill the eggs on the dog. Dips are the most economical, but they are messy. There are some effective shampoos and treatments available through pet shops and veterinarians.

Your veterinarian should be a vital part of your Boston Terrier's life. Choose a vet that is familiar with Boston Terriers and will recognize their special needs.

Another popular parasiticide is permethrin, which is applied to the back of the dog in one or two places, depending on the dog's weight. This product works as a repellent, causing the flea to get "hot feet" and jump off. Do not confuse this product with some of the organophosphates that are also applied to the dog's back.

Some products are not usable on young puppies. Treating fleas should be done under your veterinarian's guidance. Frequently, it is necessary to combine products, and the layman does not have knowledge regarding possible toxicities. It is hard to believe, but there are a few dogs that do have a natural resistance to fleas. Nevertheless, it would be wise to treat all pets at the same time. Don't forget your cats. Cats just love to prowl the neighborhood, and, consequently, return with unwanted guests.

Adult fleas live on the dog, but their eggs drop off into the environment. There, they go through four larval stages before reaching adulthood, and thereby are able to jump back on the poor unsuspecting dog. The cycle resumes and takes between 21 to 28 days under ideal conditions. There are environmental products available that will kill both adult fleas and larvae.

Ticks

Ticks can carry Rocky Mountain Spotted Fever, Lyme disease, and can cause tick paralysis. They should be removed with tweezers. Try to pull out the head because the jaws carry disease. Tick preventive collars do an excellent job. Ticks automatically back out on those dogs wearing collars.

Sarcoptic Mange

Sarcoptic mange is a mite that is difficult to find on skin scrapings. The pinnal reflex is a good indicator of this disease. Rub the ends of the pinna (ear) together and the dog will start scratching with his foot. Sarcoptes are highly contagious to other dogs and to humans, although they do not live long on humans. They cause intense itching.

There are parasites like fleas or ticks in the great outdoors, so check your dog's coat thoroughly after playing outside.

Breeding should only be done by those who are experienced and knowledgeable about the breed. Pregnant mothers need extra special care.

Demodectic Mange

Demodectic mange is a mite that is passed from the dam to her puppies. It commonly affects youngsters aged three to ten months. Diagnosis is confirmed by skin scraping. Small areas of alopecia around the eyes, lips, and/or forelegs become visible. There is little itching unless there is a secondary bacterial infection. Some breeds are afflicted more than others.

Cheyletiella

Cheyletiella causes intense itching and is diagnosed by skin scraping. It lives in the outer layers of the skin of dogs, cats, rabbits, and humans. Yellow-gray scales may be found on the back and the rump, top of the head, and the nose.

To Breed or Not To Breed

More than likely, your breeder has requested that you have your puppy neutered or spayed. Your breeder's request is based on what is healthiest for your dog and what is most beneficial for your breed. Experienced and conscientious breeders devote many years to developing a bloodline. In order to do this, they make every effort to plan each breeding cycle in regard to conformation, temperament, and health.

A responsible breeder does his or her best to perform the necessary testing (i.e., OFA, CERF, testing for inherited blood disorders, thyroid, etc.). Testing is expensive and sometimes very disheartening when a favorite dog doesn't pass his health tests. The health history pertains not only to the breeding stock, but also to the immediate ancestors. Reputable breeders do not want their offspring to be bred indiscriminately. Therefore, you may be asked to neuter or spay your puppy. Of course, there is always the exception, and the breeder may agree to let you breed your dog under his or her direct supervision. This is an important concept. More and more effort is being made to breed healthier dogs.

Spay/Neuter

There are numerous benefits to spaying or neutering your dog. Unspayed females are subject to mammary and ovarian cancer. In order to prevent mammary cancer, she must be spayed prior to her first heat cycle. Later in life, an unspayed female may develop a pyometra (an infected uterus), which is definitely life threatening.

Spaying is performed at about six months of age under a general anesthetic and is easy on the young dog. As you might expect, it is a little harder on the older dog, but that is no reason to deny her the surgery. The surgery removes the ovaries and uterus. It is important to remove all the ovarian tissue. If some is left behind, she could remain attractive to males. In order to view the ovaries, a reasonably long incision is necessary. An ovariohysterectomy is considered major surgery.

Neutering the male at a young age will inhibit some characteristic male behavior that owners frown upon. Some males will not hike their legs and mark territory if they are neutered at six months of age. Also, neutering at a young age has hormonal benefits, lessening the chance of hormonal aggressiveness.

Surgery involves removing the testicles but leaving the scrotum. If there should be a retained testicle, the male definitely needs to be neutered before the age of two or three years. Retained testicles can develop cancer. Unneutered males are at risk for testicular cancer, perineal fistulas, perianal tumors and fistulas, and prostatic disease.

Intact males and females may be prone to housetraining accidents. Females urinate frequently before, during, and after heat cycles, and males tend to mark territory if there is a female in heat. Males may show the same behavior if there is a visiting dog or guests.

Responsible breeders will screen all their Boston Terriers before breeding to ensure against genetic diseases and produce the best puppies possible.

Surgery involves a sterile operating procedure equivalent to human surgery. The incision site is shaved, surgically scrubbed, and draped. The veterinarian wears a sterile surgical gown, cap, mask, and gloves. It is customary for the veterinarian to recommend a pre-anesthetic blood screening, looking for metabolic problems, and an ECG rhythm strip to check for normal heart function. Today, anesthetics are equal to human anesthetics, which enable your dog to walk out of the clinic the same day as surgery.

Some folks worry about their dogs gaining weight after being neutered or spayed. This is usually not the case. It is true that some dogs may be less active so they could develop a problem, but most are just as active as they were before surgery. However, if your dog should begin to gain, you need to decrease his food and see to it that he gets a little more exercise.

Your Boston Terrier's eyes and nose should always look clear and clean. Notify your vet immediately if you detect any problems.

Anal Sacs

Anal sacs are small sacs on either side of the rectum that can cause the dog discomfort when they are full. They should empty when the dog has a bowel movement. Symptoms of inflammation or impaction are excessive licking under the tail and/or a bloody or sticky discharge from the anal area. Breeders recommend emptying the sacs on a regular schedule when bathing the dog. Many veterinarians prefer this isn't done unless there are symptoms. You can express the sacs by squeezing them (at the five and seven o'clock positions) in and up toward the anus. Take precautions not to get in the way of the foul-smelling fluid that is expressed. Some dogs object to this procedure, so it would be wise to have someone hold his head at this time. Sometimes you will see your dog scooting his rear end along the floor, which is caused by anal-sac irritation and not worms.

Colitis

When the stool is blood or blood tinged, it could be the result of inflammation of the colon. Colitis, sometimes intermittent, can be the result of stress, undiagnosed whipworms, or perhaps idiopathic (no explainable reason). If intermittent bloody stools are an ongoing problem, you should probably feed a diet higher in fiber. Seek professional help if your dog feels poorly and/or the condition persists.

Conjunctivitis

Many breeds are prone to conjunctivitis. The conjunctiva is the pink tissue that lines the inner surface of the eyeball, except the clear, transparent cornea. Irritating substances such as bacteria, foreign matter, or chemicals can cause it to become reddened and swollen. It is important to keep any hair trimmed from around the eyes. Long hair stays damp and aggravates the problem. Keep the eyes cleaned with warm water and wipe away any matter that has accumulated in the corner of the eyes. If the condition persists, you should see your veterinarian. This problem goes hand in hand with keratoconjunctivitis sicca.

Ear Infection

Otitis externa is an inflammation of the external ear canal that begins at the outside opening of the ear and extends inward to the

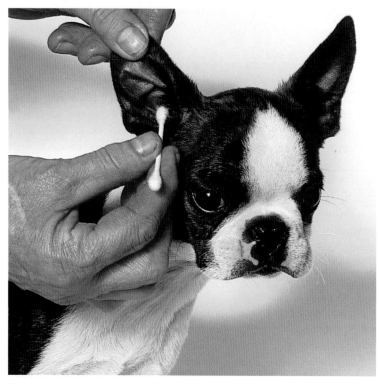

Keep your Boston Terrier's ears clean, dry, and free of any waxy buildup in order to avoid ear infections.

eardrum. Dogs with pendulous ears are prone to this disease, but breeds with upright ears also have a high incidence of problems. Allergies, food, and inhalants, along with hormonal problems, such as hypothyroidism, are major contributors to the disease. For those dogs that have recurring problems, you need to investigate the underlying causes if you hope to cure them.

Be careful never to get water in the ears. Water provides a great medium for bacteria to grow. If your dog swims or you inadvertently get water in his ears, use a drying agent. You can use an at-home preparation of equal parts of three-percent hydrogen peroxide and 70-percent rubbing alcohol. Another preparation is equal parts of white vinegar and water. Your veterinarian, alternatively, can provide a suitable product. When cleaning the ears, use cotton-tip applicators extremely carefully, because they make it easy to pack debris down into the canal. Only clean what you can see.

If your dog has an ongoing infection, don't be surprised if your veterinarian recommends sedating him and flushing his ears with a bulb syringe. Sometimes this needs to be done a few times to get the ear clean. The ear must be clean so that medication can come into contact with the canal. Be prepared to return for rechecks until the infection is gone. This may involve more flushing if the ears are very bad.

For chronic or recurring cases, your veterinarian may recommend thyroid testing, etc., and a hypoallergenic diet for a trial period of 10 to 12 weeks. Depending on your dog, it may be a good idea to see a dermatologist. Ears shouldn't be taken lightly. If the condition gets out of hand, surgery may be necessary. Please ask your veterinarian to explain proper ear maintenance for your dog.

Fleabite Allergy

Fleabite allergy is the result of a hypersensitivity to the bite of a flea and its saliva. It only takes one bite to cause the dog to chew or scratch himself raw. Your dog may need medical attention to ease

Your Boston Terrier's gait should be free and easy—he should never show any signs of pain or lameness.

If your dog is not showing his usual lively and active personality, it could indicate he isn't feeling well. Consult your veterinarian.

his discomfort. You need to clip the hair around the "hot spot" and wash it with a mild soap and water, and you may need to do this daily if the area weeps. Apply an antibiotic anti-inflammatory product. Hot spots can occur from other trauma, such as grooming.

Interdigital Cysts

Check for interdigital cysts on your dog's feet if he shows signs of lameness. They are frequently associated with staph infections and can be quite painful. A home remedy is to soak the infected foot in a solution of a half-teaspoon of bleach in a couple of quarts of water. Do this two to three times a day for a couple of days. Check with your veterinarian for an alternative remedy; antibiotics usually work well. If there is a recurring problem, surgery may be required.

Lameness

Lameness may only be an interdigital cyst or it could be a mat between the toes, especially if your dog licks his feet. Sometimes it is hard to determine which leg is affected. If your dog is holding up his leg, you need to see your veterinarian.

Skin

Frequently, poor skin is the result of an allergy to fleas, inhalants, or food. These types of problems usually result in a staph dermatitis. Dogs with food allergies usually show signs of severe itching and scratching, though some dogs with food allergies never once itch. Their only symptom is swelling of the ears with no ear infection. Food allergy may result in recurrent bacterial skin and ear infections. Your veterinarian or dermatologist will recommend a good restricted diet.

Inhalant allergies result in atopy, which causes licking of the feet, scratching the body, and rubbing the muzzle. They may be seasonable. Your veterinarian or dermatologist can perform intradermal testing for inhalant allergies. If your dog should test positive, then a vaccine may be prepared.

Tonsillitis

Usually, young dogs have a higher incidence of tonsillitis than the older ones because older dogs have built-up resistance. It is very contagious. Sometimes it is difficult to determine if the condition is tonsillitis or kennel cough because the symptoms are similar. Symptoms include fever, poor eating, swallowing with difficulty, and retching up a white, frothy mucus.

DENTAL CARE for Your Dog's Life

So, you have a new puppy! Anyone who has ever raised a puppy is abundantly aware of how this new arrival affects the household. Your puppy will chew anything he can reach, chase your shoelaces, and play "tear the rag" with any piece of clothing he can find.

When puppies are newly born, they have no teeth. At about four weeks of age, puppies of most breeds begin to develop their deciduous (baby) teeth. They begin eating semi-solid food, biting, and fighting with their littermates, and learning discipline from their mother. As their new teeth come in, they inflict pain on their mother's breasts, so feeding sessions become less frequent and shorter. By six or eight weeks, the mother will start growling to warn her pups when they are fighting too roughly or hurting her as they nurse too much with their new teeth.

Puppies need to chew. It is a necessary part of their physical and mental development. They develop muscles and necessary life skills

Providing your Boston pup with plenty of safe chew toys, like Nylabones®, will help him keep his teeth healthy.

Your Boston Terrier should have his teeth examined by the veterinarian at his regular checkup.

as they drag objects around, fight over possessions, and vocalize alerts and warnings. Puppies chew on things to explore their world. They are using their sense of taste to determine what is food and what is not. How else can they tell an electrical cord from a lizard?

At about four months of age, most puppies begin shedding their baby teeth. Often, these teeth need some help to come out to make way for the permanent teeth. The incisors (front teeth) will be replaced first. Then, the adult canine or fang teeth erupt. When a baby tooth is not shed before the permanent tooth comes in, veterinarians call it a retained deciduous tooth. This condition will often cause gum infections by trapping hair and debris between the permanent tooth and the retained baby tooth. Puppies that are given adequate chew toys will exhibit less destructive behavior, develop more physically, and have less chance of retained deciduous teeth.

During the first year, your veterinarian should see your dog at regular intervals. Your vet will let you know when to bring your puppy in for vaccinations and parasite examinations. At each visit, your vet should inspect the lips, teeth, and mouth as part of a complete physical examination.

Puppies that are given safe chew toys will exhibit less destructive behavior.

A thorough oral exam and teeth cleaning should be done as part of your dog's grooming routine.

If you give your dog good dental care throughout his lifetime, he will always be able to flash a healthy smile.

You should take some part in the maintenance of your dog's oral health. Examine your dog's mouth weekly throughout his first year to make sure there are no sores, foreign objects, tooth problems, etc. If your dog drools excessively, shakes his head, or has bad breath, consult your veterinarian. By the time your dog is six months old, his permanent teeth are all in, and plaque can start to accumulate on the tooth surfaces. This is when your dog needs good dental-care habits to prevent buildup on his teeth.

Brushing is best—that is a fact that cannot be denied. However, some dogs do not like their teeth brushed regularly, or you may not be able to accomplish the task. In this case, you should consider a product that will help prevent plaque and buildup, such as a Nylabone®.

By the time dogs are four years old, 75 percent of them have some type of periodontal disease; it is the most common infection in dogs. Yearly examinations by your vet are essential to maintaining your dog's good health. If he detects periodontal disease, he or she may recommend a prophylactic cleaning. To do a thorough cleaning, it will be necessary to put your dog under anesthesia.

With modern gas anesthetics and monitoring equipment, the procedure is fairly safe. Your veterinarian will scale the teeth with an ultrasound scaler or hand instrument. This removes the calculus from the teeth. If there are calculus deposits below the gum line, the veterinarian will plane the roots to make them smooth. After all of the calculus has been removed, the teeth are polished with pumice in a polishing cup. If any medical or surgical treatment is needed, it is done at this time. The final step would be fluoride treatment and your follow-up treatment at home. If the periodontal disease is advanced, the veterinarian may prescribe a medicated mouth rinse or antibiotics for use at home. Make sure your dog has safe, clean, and attractive chew toys, like Nylabones®, and healthy treats.

As your dog ages, professional examination and cleaning should become more frequent. The mouth should be inspected at least once a year. Your vet may recommend visits every six months. In the geriatric patient, organs such as the heart, liver, and kidneys do not function as well as when your dog was young. Your vet will probably want to test these organs' functions prior to using general anesthesia for dental cleaning.

If your dog is a good chewer and you work closely with your vet, he can keep all of his teeth all of his life. However, as your dog ages, his sense of smell, sight, and taste will diminish. He may not have the desire to chase, trap, or chew his toys. He also will not have the energy to chew for long periods, as arthritis and periodontal disease could make chewing painful. This will leave you with more responsibility for keeping his teeth clean and healthy. The dog that would not let you brush his teeth at one year of age may let you brush his teeth now that he is ten years old.

If you train your dog with good chewing habits as a puppy, he will have healthier teeth throughout his life.

T RAVELING with Your Dog

T he earlier you start traveling with your new puppy or dog, the better. He needs to become accustomed to traveling. However, some dogs are nervous riders and become carsick easily. It is helpful if he starts any trip with an empty stomach. If you continue taking him with you on short, fun rides, it will help accustom him to this experience more smoothly. How would you feel if every time you rode in the car you stopped at the doctor's office for an injection? You would soon dread that nasty car. Older dogs that tend to get carsick may have more of a problem adjusting to traveling. Those dogs that are having serious problems may benefit from medication prescribed by the veterinarian. Make sure to give your dog a chance to relieve himself before getting into the car. It is a good idea to be prepared for a clean up with a leash, paper towels, bag, and terry cloth towel.

When in the car, the safest place for your dog is in a fiberglass or wire crate, such as the Nylabone® Fold Away Pet carrier,

The Nylabone® Fold Away Pet Carrier folds up for easy storage when not in use and is great for traveling.

The Boston Terrier is an accommodating, compact dog that can accompany you anywhere you go.

although close confinement can promote carsickness in some dogs.

An alternative to the crate would be to use a car harness made for dogs and/or a safety strap attached to the harness or collar. Whatever you do, do not let your dog ride in the back of a pickup truck unless he is securely tied on a very short lead. I've seen trucks stop quickly, and, even though the dog was tied, he fell out and was dragged.

Another advantage of the crate is that it is a safe place to leave your dog if you need to run into the store. Otherwise, you wouldn't be able to leave the windows down. However, in some states, it is against the law to leave a dog in the car unattended.

Never leave a dog loose in the car wearing a collar and leash. More than one dog has killed himself by hanging. Do not let him put his head out an open window. Foreign debris can be blown into his eyes. When leaving your dog unattended in a car, consider the temperature. It can take less than five minutes to reach temperatures over 100°F.

These two future Boston champions—Hi-Society Spend'n Daddy's Money and his sister, Hi-Society Money Talks—discuss a trip with two Canadian Mounties.

Boston Terriers love to travel—they are happiest when able to participate in family activities.

TRIPS

Perhaps you are taking a trip. Give consideration to what is best for your dog—traveling with you or boarding. When traveling by car, van, or motor home, you need to think ahead about locking your vehicle. In all probability you have many valuables in the car and do not wish to leave it unlocked. Perhaps most valuable and not replaceable is your dog. Give thought to securing your vehicle and providing adequate ventilation for him. Another consideration for you when traveling with your dog is medical problems that may arise and little inconveniences, such as exposure to external parasites. Some areas of the country are quite flea infested. You may want to carry flea spray with you. This is even a good idea when staying in motels. Quite possibly you are not the only occupants of the room.

Many motels and even hotels do allow canine guests, even some very first-class ones. There are many good books available that will tell you which hotels accept dogs and also help you plan a fun vacation with your canine companion.

Call ahead to any motel that you may be considering and see if they accept pets. Sometimes it is necessary to pay a deposit against room damage. The management may feel reassured if you mention that your dog will be crated. If you do travel with your dog, take along plenty of baggies so that you can clean up after him. As a matter of fact, you should practice cleaning up everywhere you take your dog.

Depending on where you're traveling, you may need an up-to-date health certificate issued by your veterinarian. It is good policy to take along your dog's medical information, which would include the name, address, and phone number of your veterinarian, vaccination record, rabies certificate, and any medication he is taking.

AIR TRAVEL

When traveling by air, you need to contact the airlines to check their policy. Usually, you have to make arrangements up to a couple of weeks in advance when traveling with your dog. The airlines require your dog to travel in an airline-approved fiberglass crate. These can be purchased through the airlines, but they are also readily available in most pet-supply stores. The Nylabone® Fold Away Pet Carrier is a perfect crate for air travel.

If your dog is not accustomed to a crate, it is a good idea to get him acclimated to it before your trip. The day of the actual trip you should withhold serving him water for about 1 hour ahead of departure and food for about 12 hours. The airlines generally have temperature restrictions that do not allow pets to travel if it is either too cold or too hot. Frequently, these restrictions are based on the temperatures at the departure and arrival airports.

It's best to inquire about a health certificate. These usually need to be issued within ten days of departure. You should arrange for nonstop, direct flights, and if a commuter plane is involved, check to see if it will carry dogs. Some don't. The Humane Society of the United States has put together a tip sheet for airline traveling. You can receive a copy by sending a self-addressed, stamped envelope to:

The Humane Society of the United States
Tip Sheet
2100 L Street NW
Washington, DC 20037.

Regulations differ for traveling outside of the country and are sometimes changed without notice. You need to write or call the appropriate consulate or agricultural department for instructions well in advance of your trip. Some countries have lengthy quarantines (six months), and many differ in their rabies vaccination

In the event that you cannot take your dog with you, a pet sitter or boarding kennel may be an option.

requirements. For instance, it may have to be given at least 30 days ahead of your departure.

Do make sure your dog is wearing proper identification including your name, phone number, and city. You never know when you might be in an accident and separated from your dog, or your dog could be frightened and somehow manage to escape and run away.

Another suggestion would be to carry in-case-of-emergency instructions. These would include the address and phone number of a relative or friend, your veterinarian's name, address, and phone number, and your dog's medical information.

BOARDING KENNELS

Perhaps you have decided that you need to board your dog. Your veterinarian can recommend a good boarding facility or possibly a pet-sitter that will come to your house. It is customary for the boarding kennel to ask for proof of vaccination for the DHLPP, rabies, and bordetella vaccines. The bordetella should have been given within six months of boarding. This is for your protection. If they do not ask for this proof, you probably should not board at their kennel. Also ask about flea control. Those dogs that suffer fleabite allergy can get in trouble at a boarding kennel. Unfortunately, boarding kennels are limited as to how much they are able to do.

For more information on pet sitting, contact NAPPS:

National Association of Professional Pet Sitters
17000 Commerce Parkway
Suite C
Mt. Laurel, NJ 08054

Some pet clinics have technicians that pet sit and that board clinic patients in their homes. This may be an alternative for you. Ask your veterinarian if they have an employee that can help you. There is a definite advantage to having a technician care for your dog, especially if he is on medication or is a senior citizen.

You can write to the ASPCA for a copy of *Traveling With Your Pet:*

ASPCA
Education Department
424 E. 92nd Street
New York, NY 10128

IDENTIFICATION and Finding the Lost Dog

There are several ways of identifying your dog. The old standby is a collar with dog license, rabies, and ID tags. Unfortunately, collars have a way of being separated from dogs and tags fall off. We're not suggesting you shouldn't use a collar and tags. If they stay intact and on the dog, they are the quickest form of identification.

For several years, owners have been tattooing their dogs. Some tattoos use a number with a registry. Herein lies the problem, because there are several registries to check. If you wish to tattoo your dog, use your social security number. Humane shelters have the means to trace it. It is usually done on the inside of the rear thigh. The area is first shaved and numbed. There is no pain, although some dogs do not like the buzzing sound. Occasionally, tattooing is not legible and needs to be redone.

The newest method of identification is microchipping. The microchip is a computer chip that is no larger than a grain of rice.

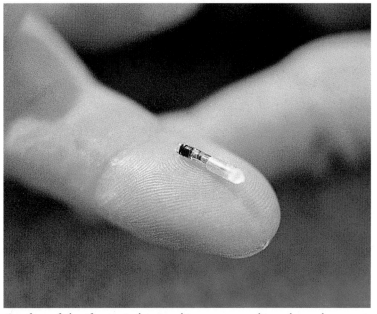

One form of identification is the microchip, a computer chip no larger than a grain of rice.

Make sure you have a clear, recent picture of your dog in case he becomes lost.

Your dog should always wear identification tags with your contact information when outside.

The veterinarian implants it by injection between the shoulder blades. The dog feels no discomfort. If your dog is lost and picked up by the humane society, they can trace you by scanning the microchip, which has its own code. Most microchip scanners are friendly to other brands of microchips and their registries. The microchip comes with a dog tag saying that the dog is microchipped. It is the safest way of identifying your dog.

FINDING THE LOST DOG

Most people would agree that losing their dog is a tragedy. Responsible pet owners rarely lose their dogs because they keep them on a leash or in an enclosed yard. However, even dogs who are in fenced-in yards can get loose. Dogs find ways to escape either over or under fences. Another fast exit may be through the gate that perhaps someone left unlocked.

Below is a list that will hopefully be of help to you if you lose your pet. Remember—don't give up; keep looking. Your dog is worth your efforts.

    1. Contact your neighbors and put flyers with a photo on it in their mailboxes. Information you should include would be

the dog's name, breed, sex, color, age, source of identification, when your dog was last seen and where, and your name and phone numbers. It may be helpful to say that the dog needs medical care. Offer a reward.

2. Check all local shelters daily. It is also possible for your dog to be picked up away from home and end up in an out-of-the-way shelter. Check these, too. Go in person. It is not enough to call. Most shelters are limited on the time they can hold dogs before they are put up for adoption or euthanized. There is the possibility that your dog will not make it to the shelter for several days. He could have been wandering or someone may have tried to keep him.

3. Notify all local veterinarians. Call and send flyers.

4. Call your breeder. Frequently, breeders are contacted when one of their dogs is found.

5. Contact the rescue group for your breed.

6. Contact local schools—children may have seen your dog.

7. Post flyers at the schools, groceries, gas stations, convenience stores, veterinary clinics, groomers, and any other places that will allow them.

8. Advertise in the newspaper.

9. Advertise on the radio.

RESOURCES

Boston Terrier Club of America, Inc.
Corresponding Secretary: Joyce Fletcher
3878 Banks Rd., Cincinnati, OH 45245
Email: candsbostons@cinci.rr.com
Website: www.bostonterrierclubofamerica.org/

American Kennel Club (AKC)
5580 Centerview Drive
Raleigh, NC 27606-9767
Phone: (919) 233-9767
Fax: (919) 233-3627
E-mail: info@akc.org
Website: www.akc.org

Association of Pet Dog Trainers (APDT)
17000 Commerce Parkway, Suite C
M. Laurel, NJ 08054
Phone: (800) PET-DOGS
Fax: (856) 439-0525
E-mail: information@adpt.com
Website: www.apdt.com

Delta Society
580 Naches Avenue SW, Suite 101
Renton, WA 98055-2297
Phone: (425) 226-7357
Fax: (425) 235-1076
E-mail: info@deltasociety.org
Website: www.deltasociety.org

States Kennel Club (SKC)
1007 W. Pine Street
Hattiesburg, MS 39401
Phone: (601) 583-8345
E-mail: skc@netdoor.com

Therapy Dogs International
88 Bartley Road
Flanders, NJ 07836
Phone: (973) 252-9800

Fax: (973) 252-7171
E-mail: tdi@gti.net
Website: www.tdi-dog.org

United Kennel Club (UKC)
100 E. Kilgore Road
Kalamazoo, MI 49002-5584
Phone: (269) 343-9020
Fax: (269) 343-7037
E-mail: hounds@ukcdogs.com
Website: www.ukcdogs.com

Canadian Kennel Club
89 Skyway Avenue, Suite 100
Etobicoke, ON M9W 6R4
Canada
Phone: (800) 250-8040 or (416) 675-5511
Fax: (416) 675-6506
E-mail: information@ckc.ca
Website: www.ckc.ca

The Kennel Club
1 Clarges Street
Piccadilly, London WIJ 8AB
England
Phone: 0870-606-6750
Fax: 020-7518-1058
Website: www.the-kennel-club.org.uk

Federation Cynologique Internationale
13 Place Albert 1er
B6530 Thuin
Belgium
Phone: ++ 32.71.59.12.38
Fax: ++ 32.71.59.22.29
E-mail: info@fci.be
Website: www.fci.be

U.S. Dog Agility Association, Inc. (USDAA)
PO Box 850955
Richardson, TX 75085-0955
Phone: (972) 487-2200
Fax: (972) 272-4404
Website: www.usdaa.com

INDEX

PHOTO CREDITS

Mary Lou Anderson, Richard Beauchamp, Bob and Eleanor Candland, Isabelle Francais, Hi-Society Boston Terriers, Great and Small Photography, JoAnne Rosenfield, K. Wheeler.